DAVID CHADWICK

HEARING
the
VOICE
of
GOD

HARVEST HOUSE PUBLISHERS
EUGENE, OREGON

Cover by Rightly Designed

HEARING THE VOICE OF GOD

Copyright © 2016 David Chadwick
Published by Harvest House Publishers
Eugene, Oregon 97402
www.harvesthousepublishers.com

ISBN 978-0-7369-6729-7 (pbk.)
ISBN 978-0-7369-6730-3 (eBook)

Library of Congress Cataloging-in-Publication Data

Names: Chadwick, David, 1949- author.
Title: Hearing the voice of God / David Chadwick.
Description: Eugene, Oregon : Harvest House Publishers, 2016. | Description based on print version record and CIP data provided by publisher; resource not viewed.
Identifiers: LCCN 2016023793 (print) | LCCN 2016019290 (ebook) | ISBN 9780736967303 () | ISBN 9780736967297 (pbk.)
Subjects: LCSH: Bible. John--Devotional literature. | Christian life--Meditations.
Classification: LCC BS2615.54 (print) | LCC BS2615.54 .C43 2016 (ebook) | DDC 242/.5—dc23
LC record available at https://lccn.loc.gov/2016023793

Printed in the United States of America

16 17 18 19 20 21 22 23 24 / BP-SK / 10 9 8 7 6 5 4 3 2 1

To all my friends and family members, especially my beloved wife, Marilynn, who have repeatedly encouraged me to try to hear God's voice in his Word, I dedicate this book.

Without you, I would have missed God's quiet whispers and loud roars in his Word.

With you, I'm reminded to listen to the voice of God regularly.

I'm eternally grateful to you.

Acknowledgments

With gratitude to my friend and editor, Steve Miller. You took a chance on me and believed I could write. You encouraged me when I didn't think my thoughts made sense. You guided me to write cogent, grammatically correct sentences. Your editorial genius has made me much better than I ever thought I could be. Thank you for everything—especially believing in me as an author.

Jesus lives in and through you. That's obvious. All who know and love you see it.

I'm honored to call you my friend and editor. I wish the world had more people like you.

If it did, it would be a much better place in which to live.

✳ ✳

Hearing What God Has to Say to You

✳ ✳ ✳

Here is a question I'm often asked: How does a person hear the voice of God? It's an important question to answer to aid people's spiritual growth. Jesus said unambiguously that his sheep hear his voice so they can know and follow him more faithfully (John 10:27).

When asked this question, I consistently give the same answer: The best way to hear God's voice is through reading, studying, and meditating on God's Word. Then the Holy Spirit will speak through those words to your heart.

I'm then asked, "Well, is there a good place to start when trying to hear God's voice in his Word?" My answer is an unequivocal yes. It's to where my dad always pointed people to start. I heard it's the same place Billy Graham encourages people to begin when reading God's Word.

It's the Gospel of John. It's a brilliant, blazing constellation of light in a world of darkness. In John, we read clear claims of Jesus' deity—more specifically, his seven "I am" statements, which are unique to the Gospel of John. John gives us deep insights into Jesus' relationship with the Father. The person and work of the Holy Spirit come alive. In John, Jesus promises us that through him, we will never hunger or thirst spiritually again.

Just when you think you know all you possibly can about Jesus, a jolt out of the Johannine blue surprises you. "Oh, I'd never seen that before!" you exclaim. Sometimes you gasp in wonder as a new revelation enlightens your heart.

I did this spiritual exercise in John for a year. Daily I would read some verses and allow my heart to be marinated by their words. I would then say, "Speak to me, Lord Jesus, in your Word." Then I'd write down what I thought the Lord was saying. It was a year of extraordinary spiritual growth.

This book, *Hearing the Voice of God*, is a compilation of that year's worth of reading, listening to, and writing down what I thought God was saying. I've now tried to translate it into a context where any reader could similarly hear God's voice in his Word.

My greatest desire is for you to experience what I experienced: God speaking powerfully and personally in his Word. While I did this over the course of a year, you're welcome to ponder and apply these readings at a pace that works best for you.

At the end of reading the Gospel of John, I hope your heart's antennae will be more finely tuned to hear God specifically speaking to you so you can follow Jesus more faithfully. Jesus said he speaks to his sheep. He yearns for his people to hear his voice and do his will, and that includes you.

I pray this devotional will aid you in hearing the voice of God as you journey through John's Gospel.

It was an incredible experience for me, and I'll never be the same because of it.

My hope is the same will be true for you.

The Gifts of Light and Life

Today's Reading: John 1:1-5

HEARING GOD'S VOICE FOR TODAY:
"He was in the beginning with God...all things were made through him...the light shines in the darkness, and the darkness has not overcome it."

* * *

Jesus existed before creation. He was with the Father when all creation was formed. Indeed, he created all things himself! There is not one atom that came into existence outside his sovereign command and control. Through him, all things came into being.

Today, as you awaken in the morning and watch the sun nod into evening, remember it's his world. When you enjoy the tantalizing tapestry, the magnificent majesty, the delightful design of his colorful creation, know that he made it all for you to richly enjoy!

He also created *you*. Before creation, he knew you by name. At the very mention of your name, his heart jumps with joy. Your name is inscribed on his heart. It is a name he will never be able to forget.

Why did Jesus create you? In eternity, the Father, and the Spirit, and the Son were in a perfect love relationship, like three distinct persons carrying out a perfectly synchronized, harmonious, and unified dance together. Jesus created you to forever dance along with them in this lavish love relationship.

He knit you together in your mother's womb. He knew the number of cells in your body, the hairs on your head, and the shape of your face. If he were to make you again, he would make you exactly as you are. You are like no other and perfect in his sight.

If your life is ever filled with darkness, please know that Jesus is not the author of darkness. In creation, he separated light from darkness. He is perfect light. His light always overcomes darkness. He is the light of the world. He is your personal light amidst all your days of darkness.

Jesus came to give you life and to give it to you abundantly. He is the author of life, not death. Choose today to live in his light and life.

As you do, trust that he oversees everything that is happening in this world. He oversees all history. He oversees your personal history. Nothing catches him by surprise. He is Lord over all. He is Lord over your life. He protects his faithful ones and promises to keep you safe.

The Lord Jesus will be with you today. He is close to the broken-hearted. He gives strength to those whose spirits are crushed. He will encourage you by giving you his strength. Nothing can separate you from his love. His personal, loving presence will be a light to all your paths.

You can trust him today.

✳ ✳

Full of Grace and Truth

Today's Reading: John 1:6-18

HEARING GOD'S VOICE FOR TODAY:
*"The Word became flesh and dwelt among us, and we have seen his
glory, glory as of the only Son from the Father, full of grace and
truth…and from his fullness we have received, grace upon grace."*

✳ ✳ ✳

Why did Jesus put on human flesh and enter your world? It's because of his great love for you. How much does he love you? He loves you so much that he put human flesh around his eternal glory and entered your world. He left the splendor of heaven to enter the squalor of a cattle trough in Bethlehem to pursue you.

If you ever doubt his love for you, remember the cradle. It's evidence of his pursuit for you. He desired to give you a new spiritual birth, to make you a child of the King of the universe! That's why he came.

The Father knew that the best way for someone to communicate with a bird would be to become a bird. And the best way for him to communicate with humans was to become human. So the Father asked the Son to put on human flesh around his glory and become one of us. Through him, you can know who God truly is and understand his eternal plan for your life.

What is Jesus' true nature? He is full of grace and truth. Never place one above the other. They are to be held in perfect tension in your life. Grace without truth becomes sloppy, mushy love—like a river with no boundaries. That produces a mosquito-laden swamp. But truth without grace becomes rigid judgmentalism. That produces death to your soul. Seek grace and truth with balance.

9

And please know that Jesus not only wants to give you grace, he wants to give you grace upon grace. The love he wants to place within you is limitless. It's beyond anything you could ever hope for or imagine.

Today, live in his grace and truth. If you have been unjustly treated, know that his truth will prevail. All will one day be held accountable for their actions. And he oversees all human history. No one gets away with anything. Trust his perfect justice.

And let your heart be filled with his grace upon grace. Know the extent to which the Father would go to pursue you and fill with you with his love. He yearns to be one with you forever—his heart inextricably linked with yours for all eternity. He loves deeply those who love him.

And should you choose to continue to run away from Jesus, he will continue to pursue you with grace upon grace. He loves you that much.

The proof of his love is evidenced in the cradle—the fact that he came to you. He put on human flesh and pursued you.

You were that important to him.

You always will be.

✳ ✳

Who Are You?

Today's Reading: John 1:19-28

HEARING GOD'S VOICE FOR TODAY:
*"This is the testimony of John, when the Jews sent priests and
Levites from Jerusalem to ask him, 'Who are you?' He confessed,
and did not deny, but confessed, 'I am not the Christ.'"*

✳ ✳ ✳

Anyone who speaks in support of Jesus will face opposition. Sometimes you'll feel lonely, like a voice crying in the wilderness. John the Baptist did. So will you.

Everyone who says they follow Jesus has a testimony about him. The question is what kind of testimony it is. What is yours? Is it silent? Is it indifferent? Is it consistent? Is it passionate? Is it unabashed?

John was asked, "Who are you?" The same question should be asked of you. "Who are you?" Your answer goes far beyond your name, background, position, power, or people's approval. God never calls people to be famous, but faithful.

Who are you? This is a question about your identity. Is it found solely in Jesus and him alone? If you find your identity in anything other than Jesus, it will fade like the morning dew on the grass. It's a vanishing vapor and will not last.

John answered "Who are you?" by saying, "I am not the Christ." He knew his purpose in life was not to be Jesus but to point people to him. Belonging completely to the Lord was his purpose in life. Can you say the same thing about yourself?

John simply wanted people to know Jesus. He said he wasr'

worthy to put his fingers on the straps of Jesus' dirty, grungy sandals and untie them.

Today, examine your heart. Is there a desire within you for self-exaltation and self-aggrandizement? Do you proudly think you are worthy to untie Jesus' sandals? Be honest. Place your life as a mirror against his selfless, sacrificial life. See in the Son the Father's intention for all humanity. See in Jesus his desire for all humans to serve, not be served, to be servants, not superstars. Loving others proves you are one of his disciples and his love lives in you.

The Father desires your life to be spent pointing people to him, not yourself. He wants your life to be a testimony to his greatness, not your own.

You are not the Christ. Quit trying to control others and your world. Give it all to him. He oversees all. He controls all. You don't. Trust him today with everything in your life.

Is God like a human who changes his mind? Has he ever spoken and failed to act? Has he ever promised anything and not carried through? Of course not!

John knew this truth.

Do you?

The Spirit Remains

Today's Reading: John 1:29-34

HEARING GOD'S VOICE FOR TODAY:
*"And John bore witness: 'I saw the Spirit descend from
heaven like a dove, and it remained on him.'"*

✳ ✳ ✳

When John the Baptist saw Jesus walking toward him, John exclaimed that he is the Lamb of God who takes away the sins of the world. He foresaw Christ's substitutionary death on the cross for all the world's sins to be forgiven.

That includes your sins as well. No matter what you've done, if you confess your sins to him and ask for forgiveness, you are forever forgiven. His Spirit enters your heart. You now have a personal relationship with Jesus for all eternity. He promises that he will never leave you or forsake you.

This promise was evidenced when John baptized Jesus. As he did so, the Spirit descended from heaven and remained upon Jesus and in him. During every moment of Jesus' earthly ministry, the Spirit empowered his life and obedience to his Father in heaven. Their hearts were interlocked in perfect union. The Spirit never left him. He was always with him—no matter what temptation or trial he would face.

When you receive Jesus as the perfect Lamb of God who takes away the sins of the world, the same Holy Spirit who remained with and in him will remain with and in you as well. There is no sin you can ever commit to cause him to leave you. He will be with you constantly no matter what temptation or trial you may face. He is God's promised presence for all his children who believe in Jesus.

The Spirit empowers your life to be a witness for Jesus. He abides in you and causes a perfect union life between you and the Lord.

Today, no matter what you are facing, know you face it with Jesus' presence in you. He will confront all your problems with you, comforting you with his strength and encouraging your heart to persevere and never give up. He is for you. He is on your side. He will constantly whisper to your heart that all will work together for your good and his glory.

Jesus will guide you forever. Until your last day on earth, he will be your eternal presence. He directs the steps of the godly. He will show you the proper path, even if you should go astray. He delights in overseeing every detail of your life.

Jesus' life is in you. Your life is in him. You are forever enjoined as one. He has baptized you with his Holy Spirit. Make your plans today. But know Jesus determines your steps. He will guide you along the best pathway for your life. He will advise and watch over you. Hold his right hand. Trust he is leading you. That should bring his perfect peace to your heart.

You can trust Jesus today.

What Are You Seeking?

Today's Reading: John 1:35-42

HEARING GOD'S VOICE FOR TODAY:
"What are you seeking?...Come and you will see."

∗ ∗ ∗

Andrew and John (the writer of this Gospel) were two of John the Baptist's disciples. But when John pointed out that Jesus was the Lamb of God who takes away the world's sins, they started to follow him.

Andrew and John spent the day with Jesus. As with any meaningful and personal friendship, you can't really know Jesus unless you spend regular time with him.

During this time together, Jesus asked them a very important question to ponder. It was not just for them, but for you as well. "What are you seeking?" he asked. Everyone is seeking after something in life. What are you seeking? Fame? Popularity? Significance? Prestige? Influence?

Jesus then invited them to come and see. He invited them to explore his claims and teachings. He invited them to come and see true purpose in life.

Jesus did this because he knew that if someone truly tries to seek him, they will find him. Every spiritual seeker and skeptic who explores honestly who Jesus is will eventually discover the truth about him. They will find him. They will enter into a personal relationship with him. They will find the true purpose of life.

What are you seeking in life? Has it completely filled the vacuum of your heart? Or has it left you feeling empty and purposeless?

When Andrew realized who Jesus was, he excitedly found his brother Cephas to tell him whom he'd discovered. He introduced Cephas to the Lord, who saw his future and knew his faith would become the bedrock of his church. Jesus didn't see who Cephas was, but who he'd become. He renamed him Peter, the rock. He knew his glorious destiny. And he used Peter to change the world.

When you find Jesus, you can't wait to tell others about him. You know you've found life's purpose in him. You want others to know him as well.

Today, continue to come to Jesus with all your burdens. Continue to seek him with all your heart. Continue to pursue his purpose for you.

Know that Jesus doesn't see your present messiness. He sees your future. It is filled with hope! He sees you as a rock of faith, someone who can influence countless others for him. He sees you as a world-changer for him. See yourself as Jesus sees you.

Don't ever doubt it. It's true! Jesus wants to give you a great future and hope.

Just make sure you always come and seek after Jesus—his kingdom and righteousness. Everything else will be naturally added to you.

✳ ✳

Follow Me

Today's Reading: John 1:43-51

HEARING GOD'S VOICE FOR TODAY:
*"He found Philip and said to him, 'Follow me.'…Nathanael
said to him, 'How do you know me?' Jesus answered him, 'Before
Philip called you, when you were under the fig tree, I saw you.'"*

✳ ✳ ✳

There are two great truths Jesus reveals to us here. They are found in how he called two of his disciples.

First, look at how Jesus called Philip. He found him in Galilee and simply said to him, "Follow me." Jesus didn't call Philip to follow a set of rules and regulations. No, he called him to follow himself. Jesus invited Philip to live as he lived—to emulate him and let his life flow through him. He would change Philip from the inside/out. That's what would happen as he followed Jesus, who calls you to follow him as well.

Second, note that Philip went and found his friend Nathanael. He told him he had found the Messiah, the one to whom the Law and prophets pointed.

Initially, Nathanael doubted Jesus. He had heard Jesus was from Nazareth. He didn't think anything good could come from Nazareth. His heart was filled with prejudice.

When Nathanael finally did come, Jesus already felt great love toward him. He knew what was in Nathanael's heart—even his prejudice. Before Nathanael ever approached Jesus, Jesus supernaturally saw him sitting under a fig tree—a symbol for the nation of Israel. Nathanael was struggling with why God's people had wandered so far from the Father's intentions. Why were they under Roman occupation and oppression?

Nathanael's heart was seeking truth. He didn't know that God's truth was already seeking him. Before Nathanael ever came to Jesus, the Lord already knew him and his heart. Long before he ever chose Jesus, Nathanael had already been chosen to follow him. Before Nathanael ever loved Jesus, the Lord first loved him.

Jesus was waiting to replace Nathanael's prejudice with his unconditional love.

Today, know that Jesus wants you to follow him. Your life is found in him. With everything you face today, simply follow him. Imitate him. Do what he calls you to do. Listen to his still, small voice within you. He will lead and guide you.

And know how much Jesus loves you. He loved you before this world was created. He knows all your struggles, doubts, questions, prejudices, and meanderings. Even while you were sinning, Jesus had chosen to die on the cross to forgive your sins.

He saw you before you ever saw him. He chose to love you before you ever chose to love him. You can't begin to imagine what Jesus has prepared for you.

Rest in these realities today…and forever.

✳ ✳

The Best Till Last

Today's Reading: John 2:1-12

HEARING GOD'S VOICE FOR TODAY:
*"My hour has not yet come...But you have
kept the good wine until now."*

✳ ✳ ✳

This is Jesus' first recorded miracle. It occurred at a wedding feast in Cana, a city in Galilee.

Jesus' mother, Mary, had become concerned because the feast had run out of wine. This was potentially a humiliating embarrassment for her friends. So she came to Jesus and stated, very simply, "They have no wine."

Mary knew deep in her soul how special Jesus was. From her cousin Elizabeth sharing how her son, John, leapt in her womb when Mary entered the room with Jesus in hers, to the shepherds coming to the manger in adoration of her newly born baby boy, to the wise men arriving and offering expensive gifts to him, she knew Jesus was special. So she turned to him in this time of need.

In response, Jesus said, "My hour has not yet come." He wasn't being insensitive. He knew miracles might push a messianic expectation that was not yet ready to be realized. The Jews wanted a military leader to eradicate Roman oppression. Instead, Jesus offered to die for their sins. It was not yet his time to reveal this truth and go to the cross.

But Jesus did meet her and others' needs. His heart was moved with compassion. He changed the water into wine. In fact, his wine was so much better that the guests assumed the best wine had been saved until the end of the feast—not the way things were done!

Trust today that Jesus has a perfect hour for everything in your life. As you wait for him to act on his promises, wait patiently. All times and hours are in his hands. If it's not yet the hour for him to act for you, continue to trust him. His timing is always perfect.

Also, know that Jesus cares about the most intimate concerns of your life. Even your hidden feelings of embarrassment and humiliation are of concern to him. Come to him today and give them to him—no matter how great or small. Let him carry them for you. He cares about everything in your life.

Finally, even as you grow older, please know how much he still cares for you. He saves his best wine until the end. He saves people's best years in life to be their last years. Age is just a number. It means nothing to him. All he cares about is your faithfulness. He wants to use your later years in great ways for his glory.

Give him the rest of your life. Give him all your years today. He ordered them all. He cares about every second of your life on earth. Great is his faithfulness.

Your best is yet to come.

* *

Live on Purpose

Today's Reading: John 2:13-17

HEARING GOD'S VOICE FOR TODAY:
*"Take these things away; do not make
my Father's house a house of trade."*

* * *

When Jesus entered the Temple, he became angry about how it was being used. Merchants and money-changers were selling animals to the pilgrims coming to Jerusalem from all over the Roman Empire. These animals were offered by the pilgrims as sacrifices to God to receive his forgiveness. People were using his holy place of worship to make money. Jesus' soul was grieved. And his anger increased.

But his anger was especially aroused as Jesus observed that this hypocrisy was happening in the court of Gentiles. This outer court was where Gentile spiritual seekers would gather and ask about how to worship God.

But all the commotion caused by the merchants kept the Gentiles from knowing the Lord. The Temple had been built, as Isaiah said, to be a house of prayer for all the nations (Isaiah 56:7). That's why God had instructed Kings David and Solomon to build it. It was intended to be a place for Jew and Gentile alike to come and worship the Father.

What does this mean for you today? Remember that your body is the temple of the Holy Spirit. In you he lives and moves and has his being. And it's through you and your life that those who don't know him will have an opportunity to find him. You are presently his house of prayer for all the nations. People look to you to know him.

Therefore, remove anything that keeps Jesus from fully indwelling you. Eliminate specifically everything that may keep those who don't know him from seeing him in your life. Take away all hatred, lusts, consumerism, materialism, wrath, anger, bitterness, slander, malice, despair, discouragement, disappointment, and hopelessness.

In anger, Jesus swept the Temple clean because of his zeal for God's house.

Similarly, he has a zeal for you. He is jealous for your affection in return. He doesn't want anything to keep you two from being close. He doesn't want to share you with any other affection you may have. Other loves can quickly and easily replace your love for him and become idols. Don't let it happen. Sweep away these things. Don't let your life be simply for commerce, trade, and making money.

Jesus wants you to live on purpose. As he came to seek and save that which was lost, he desires you to do the same. When people who don't know him see your "temple" cluttered with the things of this world, they won't desire to know him. Get rid of all the stuff! Have an eternal perspective. Live for Jesus' eternal rewards. Everything else is considered worthless in comparison to the infinite value of knowing him.

Make Jesus the master passion of your life. Seek first his kingdom. Make the doing of his will what you desire most in this world. Make sure you pray regularly for all the nations to come to faith in Jesus.

And he will use you in others' lives in ways you never dreamed possible.

✳ ✳

People Make Lousy Gods

Today's Reading: John 2:18-25

HEARING GOD'S VOICE FOR TODAY:

*"Destroy this temple, and in three days I will raise it
up...But Jesus on his part did not entrust himself to
them, because...he himself knew what was in man."*

✳ ✳ ✳

After Jesus cleansed the Temple, he was not very popular. The religious authorities demanded that he give them a sign to validate his authority. His answer pointed to his resurrection. "Destroy this temple, and in three days I will raise it up," he declared to them. As Creator over this world, he knew he had the power to resurrect his physical body. He knew he would return from the grave.

Today, believe that if you trust in Jesus, you will be raised from the dead as well. After death, you will receive a glorious, eternal, flawless resurrection body. You will never die. Rather, you will step from this life into the next one.

It is a day to which you should look forward. It should allow you to face today without fear or anxiety. Where is the fear of death? Where is its victory? It's been swallowed up in the reality of your future resurrection from the grave.

And if Jesus controls your life after death, he will surely control your life today. Nothing that happens to you is beyond his control. Don't fear! No weapon formed against you will prosper. He is your God. He upholds you with all his strength. Face today with courage and boldness.

And as you do, remember not to put your faith in people. Resist every ounce of living life trying to please people!

Jesus did. He didn't trust anyone. Why? Because he knew what was in every person's heart. He knew what motivated people. He knew the pernicious pride that indwells every person. He knew that every human primarily looks out for number one. He knew that everyone has an inbuilt desire for the world to revolve around him and use other people for their own personal, selfish benefits.

Jesus is trying to teach us the dangers of living for the praises of people. He knew how fickle they are. He knew the power of sin in their hearts and how self-serving they are. Therefore, he entrusted himself to no one. He trusted God alone. He knew steadfast, eternal joy could never be found in people's ever-changing whims and fancies.

Jesus later experienced this truth. As he died on the cross, all the disciples, except John, deserted him. They were afraid they'd be captured and killed in a similar fashion.

Today, realize that people make lousy gods. Don't trust them. If you depend upon them, you will be disappointed.

Depend solely on Jesus. Trust explicitly in him. He will never leave nor forsake you.

He will never let go of you. He will never give up on you. His love never fails.

✳ ✳

You Must Be Born Again

Today's Reading: John 3:1-14

HEARING GOD'S VOICE FOR TODAY:
"Truly, truly I say to you, unless one is born again he cannot see the kingdom of God…That which is born of the Spirit is spirit."

✳ ✳ ✳

You must be born again by the Holy Spirit to see and experience God's kingdom. It's not merely optional. It's essential for eternal life. You *must* be born again through the Holy Spirit.

Before sin entered the world, God's first created children, Adam and Eve, walked in perfect harmony with him in the Garden of Eden. Nothing hindered their relationship with him.

When they declared their independence from the Father by eating of the tree of the knowledge of good and evil, selfishness entered their hearts. Separation occurred between them and their Father. Their hearts became dead. There was no longer any kingdom rule from God in them.

Sadly, the rebellious sin nature within them has now been passed on to everyone who has ever been born. All human hearts are dead in their sins and trespasses.

Jesus came to earth to reestablish the Father's personal, loving, intimate relationship with humanity. He came to reestablish his kingdom rule and eternal presence in all hearts. The forgiveness he offers on the cross is intended for the Holy Spirit to flood people's hearts with his overwhelming love, mercy, and kindness. Where the human heart was once bent toward self, the new spiritual birth causes hearts to be bent toward God's loving, inward kingdom rule and others.

Has this new birth happened in you? It's easy to know. Do you desire to do God's will? Do you want God's eternal kingdom to rule in your heart? Have you inwardly experienced the breadth, width, and height of his forgiving grace? Do you love to worship him and pray to him—living every moment in joyful thanksgiving and praise for the new life within you?

When you have been spiritually reborn, you know that Jesus lives inside you through the Holy Spirit. He abides permanently in your heart. You are a new creation. Your sins are forgiven and forgotten. You are certain that Jesus is an eternal amnesiac.

You know Jesus will be with you for all of your days on earth. You know you can place all your burdens on his shoulders because he is strong and able to carry them. You can know with certainty that he cares for you. You are indelibly and inextricably connected to him now and for eternity. Isn't this wonderful news?

And the seeking of his kingdom is now the master passion of your life. Those who desire to do Jesus' will are his family.

Does this describe you? Have you been born again?

It must happen for you to be a member of God's kingdom.

✳ ✳

God's Great Love

Today's Reading: John 3:15-21

HEARING GOD'S VOICE FOR TODAY:
*"For God so loved the world, that he gave his only Son, that
whoever believes in him should not perish but have eternal life."*

✳ ✳ ✳

Child of God, see the Father's love for you in each phrase in this verse.

"For God so loved the world..." The Father's covenant love is for everyone in the world. All people everywhere are objects of this love. How is this love known?

"That he gave his only Son..." The Father's love is not mere flabby, fluffy feelings. It's a specific action. Real love is a verb. The Father sent Jesus, his only beloved Son, to earth as a man. He put on human flesh and went to the cross to bear the penalty for your sin upon his body—something he didn't deserve. When you accept his gift of eternal life, you receive the Father's glorious righteousness—something you don't deserve. All this was done for you because of the Father's great love for you.

"That whoever believes in him..." This grand statement is for anyone who will humbly believe in Jesus and receive his gift of eternal life. No one is excluded from this offer.

"Should not perish..." This is the "bad news" of the gospel. You can never fully appreciate the good news of Jesus' gift of eternal life until you understand the bad news of the inevitability of eternal separation from the Father because of your sin. The Father is pure and holy. No sin dwells in him. Any sinful person trying to enter his presence must be rejected. As a healthy body rejects unhealthy germs, so God rejects sin from his presence. It's what his holy nature must do. People are doomed to perish without his forgiveness.

"But have eternal life…" The Father in heaven desires no one to perish and be rejected from his presence at death. That's why Jesus came to earth and put on human flesh. He came to seek and save that which was lost. He came to rescue the perishing and give them the free gift of eternal life.

When you clearly know what you are saved from, and what you are saved for, you will never doubt Jesus' eternal love. You know he will be with you daily until you come home to be with him forever.

Does the "whoever" in this verse describe you? Do you believe Jesus died on the cross to forgive you of your sins? Have you accepted his free gift of eternal life?

If so, you can face today with confidence no matter what may come your way. Jesus will be with you as you face it. You have eternal life, and this life is found in Jesus.

When you believed in Jesus, you came into fellowship with the Son and the Father. And you now enjoy the eternal life Jesus promised you. Your eternal destiny is secure. He is always with you.

Because this is true, why worry about anything you may face today?

✳ ✳

The Importance of Humility

Today's Reading: John 3:22-36

HEARING GOD'S VOICE FOR TODAY:
"He must increase, but I must decrease."

✳ ✳ ✳

This verse shows Jesus' special and personal relationship with John the Baptist. It expresses why they were very close. It shows why Jesus loved him. It's what Jesus wants all relationships with him to be like.

Jesus must increase. You must decrease.

For this to happen, your willingness to decrease must be a daily choice. It means you desire to lessen your own importance and glorify Jesus. When you glorify someone, you render a good opinion of him. When you glorify Jesus, you render a good opinion of him in the eyes of others. Personal glory decreases. His glory increases. Through the lens of your life's camera, you desire to render a good opinion of Jesus as people see him living in and through you.

Is Jesus first in your life? Is he preeminent in who you are and all you do? Do you desire his kingdom to be first in your life and then trust he will bring to you everything else you need—in his time and in his way?

Anything penultimate in your life is an idol. Jesus must be ultimate.

You are never to use Jesus for your own glory. Rather, he is to use you for his glory. All that you have, all that you own, all the successes you've known, are all because he has chosen to give them to you. Everything you have in life—from your family to friends to the clothes you wear—are gifts from him to you. They come to you solely because of his grace.

This is especially true of your sins being forgiven and your personal relationship with Jesus. You are forgiven solely because of his grace. If you could work your way to your own salvation, you'd brag about it forever. Heaven would forever hear the echoes of your boastful words that earned the Lord's favor. But you didn't. You can't. Your eternal relationship with Jesus is a magnanimous gift from him to you—unearned and by grace.

All you have in life comes from him. The proof that you know this is your heartfelt willingness to humbly and daily say, "He must increase. I must decrease."

That was John the Baptist's passion. Is it yours? It should be.

When it's true, you will give him control of every area of your life. You will live every day in joyful, thankful, and humble worship of him—giving him all the glory in everything. You are like a little child whom Jesus said is the greatest in his kingdom.

You will decrease. And he will increase.

That's God's will for your life—today and all days.

✳ ✳

Eternal Water

Today's Reading: John 4:1-15

HEARING GOD'S VOICE FOR TODAY:
"Everyone who drinks of this water will be thirsty again, but whoever drinks of the water that I will give him will never be thirsty again. The water I will give him will become to him a spring of water welling up to eternal life."

✳ ✳ ✳

When Jesus talked with the Samaritan woman at the well, he wanted her to know why he had left heaven and come to earth. He came to satisfy the deepest longings of the human heart. He came for her and you to drink his eternal water that satisfies the soul forever.

She misunderstood Jesus' initial teaching. She thought he was speaking about drawing literal water from the town well. She was hoping Jesus would help make her daily manual labor easier.

Too many people think that way as well. They are longing for earthly realities to satisfy their eternal souls. They fail to understand the spiritual, eternal world of which Jesus speaks and teaches.

But Jesus came to earth to birth within people a new spiritual, eternal life. He came to place a well of living spiritual water within their souls so they would never thirst again. This living water is the Holy Spirit—the third person of the Godhead.

When the Holy Spirit is invited to indwell your heart, Jesus' eternal presence of limitless love bubbles up and overwhelms you. His plan and purpose for your life is revealed. Life has new meaning.

There are two kingdoms surrounding you—an earthly one and a heavenly one. The Lord's kingdom is not of this world. His kingdom is gloriously eternal. This earthly kingdom is temporary and transient. It is fading away, along with what people crave.

Jesus' eternal kingdom will last forever. You enter it when your heart is born of the Spirit—his living water drenching your parched soul. It is an eternal well that rises up and overflows your soul. Only this living water can satisfy your deepest longings.

That's what Jesus was trying to teach this woman. And that's what he wants you to know today. As the deer pants for water, Jesus wants your soul to long for his living water.

Are you a citizen of his eternal kingdom? Do you know the reality of his living water within you? Are you allowing your deepest longings to be met solely by his spiritual life inside you? Or are you still seeking meaning in the tawdry, temporary realities of this world?

From the time Jesus entered you, his eternal grace, mercy, and kindness grows. He removes your stony, stubborn heart and gives you a tender, responsive heart. You rest in his strength. Your dry soul is renewed by his presence. You belong to him. You are his prized possession. He is yours. You are his.

Let Jesus' living water flow in and through your life today. He will satisfy your heart's every longing. He will overwhelm you with his love.

That's his promise to you.

✳ ✳

True Worshipers

Today's Reading: John 4:16-26

HEARING GOD'S VOICE FOR TODAY:
*"The hour is coming, and is now here, when the true worshipers
will worship the Father in spirit and truth, for the Father is
seeking such people to worship him. God is spirit and those
who worship him must worship him in spirit and truth."*

✳ ✳ ✳

When the Spirit indwells your heart and you know Jesus' overflowing love, worship is not something you do weekly or only during special holy seasons. Worship is a lifestyle. It's not something you do. It's who you are.

You can worship Jesus while washing dishes. Or when you are working in front of a computer. Or when you are parenting. Or when you are selling real estate. Whatever you are doing becomes worship if it's done for his glory.

Worship is the daily emphasis of Jesus' preeminence in every area of your life.

The Father is spirit—not a physical body. He is not limited to one place in the world. When he lives inside you, you can worship him at any time and in any place.

There are two requirements for a true worshiper. First, he must be filled with the Holy Spirit. The Spirit lives in the heart of the worshiper who confesses Jesus as Lord and Savior. The Lord is regularly present in his life.

Second, he must be committed to the truth. There must be a commitment to and love of the Word of God—the Father's written truth on earth. In the Upper Room, right before Jesus' death, he prayed this prayer to his Father for all his disciples: "Sanctify them in the truth, your word is truth" (John 17:17).

Does his Spirit totally indwell your inner life? Does he control every area of your life? Is there anything in your life you value more than him? Are you committed to his Word as complete truth? Is his Word your only infallible rule of faith and practice in every area of your life?

Let Jesus have first place in your life today. Let his life gurgle within you and control all. Abide in him, and he will abide in you. If you draw near to him, he will draw near to you. Honor him, and he will honor you. Yield all your life to him. Love his Word. It is true.

When you do, you will praise the One who has shown you his unfailing love. You will know it's good to give thanks to him and worship his name. You will know that God is worthy to receive all glory, honor, and power. He created all things, and they exist because he created what he pleased. He is worthy of all our praise.

When you know who God truly is, you become a true worshiper of him—no matter where you may be.

And that's his master passion for your life.

✳ ✳

Lift Up Your Eyes

Today's Reading: John 4:27-38

HEARING GOD'S VOICE FOR TODAY:
*"I have food you know nothing about...Look, I tell you, lift
up your eyes, and see that the fields are white for harvest."*

✳ ✳ ✳

Jesus' disciples went into the village to get something to eat. They returned and offered some food to him. He refused it.

They were confused. They had traveled a long distance. They knew Jesus was hungry. They urged him to eat. But he used this moment to teach them something important.

Jesus used the physical food they offered to him to teach them an eternal reality. The most important food they would ever ingest was not physical food, but to do the will of his Father. That's what fueled Jesus' life. It needed to fuel theirs as well.

What was that "food" that gave his life an eternal perspective and purpose? It was the harvesting of people's eternal souls. He came to earth to seek and save people who were lost (Luke 19:10).

This world has farming seasons dotting the calendar year that lead to eventual harvests. Similarly, human souls have spiritual seasons when they are more ready to be harvested into the kingdom.

For you to be a part of this harvest, you need to lift up your eyes and see people all around you who need God's grace and forgiveness. They surround you.

But so many human eyes are looking inward—concerned only with their own life's situations and problems. Or they are looking downward—discouraged and depressed. Or they are looking at others—unceasingly panting to impress and please other people.

Jesus wants you to join his mission. How? By looking up. By being aware of the numbers of people in your sphere of influence and around the world who need his grace and forgiveness. The fields around you are white for harvest.

The harvest is plentiful but the laborers are few. Please join him.

Today, pray for the Lord's inner promptings to lead you to someone who needs him. Listen carefully to his voice. His followers can hear his voice. Then go to that person. Offer a helping hand. Listen to his hurting heart. Pray for Jesus to open a door where you can share how he has touched your life. No one can ever refute your testimony.

Then share the truth of who Jesus is. Don't be concerned about the possibility they may reject you. Always remember this truth: You are in sales; the Lord is in management. It's your job to share about him. Yes, you need to offer to people the chance to respond to the gospel. But realize it's God's job to bring them to himself. All the pressure is gone!

Join Jesus in the most exciting adventure you can possibly imagine—pointing people to him and seeing their eternal trajectory changed.

You'll find purpose in life like never before.

God's Love for Everyone

Today's Reading: John 4:39-45

HEARING GOD'S VOICE FOR TODAY:
"They said to the woman, 'It is no longer because of what you said that we believe, for we have heard for ourselves, and we know that this is indeed the Savior of the world.'"

✳ ✳ ✳

Jesus spent two days in Samaria. During this time, the woman whom he had met at the well told all her friends about him. They came in large numbers to hear him teach eternal realities. After hearing about Jesus' identity, they came to know him personally as their Lord and Savior. They understood his earthly mission. They believed in him, and he forgave their sins.

At that moment, Jesus' earthly disciples were able to receive a glimpse of the worldwide harvest that would come after his death and resurrection. He had come to die for the sins of all people in the world—even the Samaritans.

That was difficult for his disciples to understand. The Jews despised the Samaritans. They thought them unworthy of God's love and acceptance.

But when Jesus' disciples saw that he loved the hated Samaritans, they began to comprehend that his love was for everyone in the world. They came to realize that God's forgiving love was to be extended to everyone everywhere, for all need a Savior.

How about you? Do you know Jesus as your personal Savior? Do you know of his extraordinary grace, mercy, and forgiveness for you?

Do you know that he doesn't despise you? Do you know how valuable and priceless you are in his sight?

If so, you know that he doesn't see you as guilty anymore. You aren't filthy anymore. He's not angry with you. He is your personal Savior. He has saved you from your sins and forgiven you. He has given you eternal life—solely by his grace. He has placed his boundless love in your heart.

Jesus came to this earth to seek and save the lost—including despised Samaritans—and all who are lost and aimlessly wandering without hope. And people like you.

Receive his love anew today. He will satisfy all your deepest longings within you. He will heal your hurts. He will rest in you forever. He will carry your burdens. You will never face anything without his eternal power and presence with you.

Believe today that Jesus is for you. He is on your side. He doesn't remember your sins anymore. You should never feel condemnation. His grace is sufficient for you.

In your weakness, Jesus is strong. Through him, you can do anything because he indwells you and gives you the strength to face it.

He is your Savior.

That's the best news you will ever hear.

✳ ✳

Miracles Still Happen

Today's Reading: John 4:46-52

HEARING GOD'S VOICE FOR TODAY:

"The official said to him, 'Sir, come down before my child dies.'
Jesus said to him, 'Go; for your son will live.' The man believed
the word that Jesus spoke to him and went on his way...So he
asked them the hour when he began to get better, and they said
to him, 'Yesterday at the seventh hour the fever left him.'"

✳ ✳ ✳

Why are miracles so hard for people to believe? Every miracle is rooted in Genesis 1:1: "In the beginning, God created the heavens and the earth." With one simple word, creation occurred. From nothing, creation came.

If God created all, doesn't he control all? Can't he work within his creation to do as he wishes? If he made everything, can't he give people a miracle if he wishes?

A certain Roman official came to Jesus to ask him to go to his home and heal his son. He simply believed Jesus was able to do it. The Lord saw his great faith. He told the official that his son was alive. The official "simply believed" in Jesus' word, and returned home.

As he made his way home, he met his servants who were coming for him. This Roman official was a good man. He treated his servants well. They told him his son's fever had broken. He asked the exact time when it happened. When told, he knew it was the same moment Jesus had told him that the fever had departed.

Believe today that God is able to do exceedingly more than you could ever ask or imagine. Nothing is impossible for him. He created you. He formed every part of you in your mother's womb. He oversaw every interconnected cell in your body. He is the God of all flesh. Nothing is too hard for him because he created everything.

Come to him with your needs, burdens, cares, hurts, and disappointments. Like the Roman official and father who deeply cared for his son, come to him and ask, seek, and knock. Have faith in God and don't doubt. Be confident that what we hope for will happen. Faith gives us assurance about things we can't see. It's impossible to please God without faith. He rewards those who diligently seek him.

Today, do you need a miracle? Ask God for anything. Whether your need is great or small, make your requests known to him. He cares intimately about every area of your life—and the lives of your children and loved ones. If he knows the number of hairs on your head and when a sparrow falls to the ground, he certainly knows and cares for you—the crown of his creation.

God controls everything in this world. He controls everything in your life. He controls the exact hour when a healing happens. He oversees all. He is the God of the miraculous.

Tell him what you need. Ask him for a miracle. You have not because you ask not. Trust that he loves you. Lay it in his hands. Believe that he has the best answers for your requests.

Miracles are not difficult for him.

✳ ✳

Have Faith in God

Today's Reading: John 4:53-54

Hearing God's Voice for Today:
"He himself believed, and all his household. This was the second sign that Jesus did when he had come from Judea to Galilee."

✳ ✳ ✳

God is the God of miracles. When Jesus spoke, the Roman official's son was healed. It happened at the exact hour he ordained. He oversees all times and seasons.

The Roman official believed in Jesus. He completely trusted him. He knew that he oversees all in the universe. He knew Jesus oversaw his son's life.

The healing of the official's son was the second miracle Jesus did in Cana of Galilee. The first was when he changed water into wine at the wedding feast. Miracles went on to become a common practice in his ministry.

Why did Jesus perform miracles? He used them as signs to point people to himself. They were means to the end of helping individuals come to faith in him. They were evidence that the kingdom of God had come to earth. They were proof that Jesus was God's Son sent to earth to die for the forgiveness of people's sins.

Ask the Lord for a miracle today. He still does them. Believe that he is able to give it to you. He is the Alpha and the Omega—the beginning and the end. He is the first and the last—Lord over all history. He spoke, and the world was created. He spoke, and the Roman official's son was healed.

Ask him to speak into the tough times in your life today. If you have the faith of a mustard seed, you can speak to a mountain and demand it be moved. Nothing becomes impossible. Ask him to create something from your nothing in your life. Believe he is able. He is.

And when you see him move in your life, trust him even more! Believe that you never need to fear anything. Believe he can supply anything you may need.

Give Jesus your cares. He is especially concerned for your children—as he was with the Roman official's son. Trust him with their burdens. Believe he wants to touch them—even if they have wandered far away from him. Keep praying for them. Don't give up! A parent's prayer has prolific power in eternity. Believe they will soon return to him.

Give Jesus everything—your concerns large and small, personal and familial. He cares for them all. None of your concerns is beyond his help.

He still does miracles.

Just have faith in God.

Do You Want to Be Healed?

Today's Reading: John 5:1-9

HEARING GOD'S VOICE FOR TODAY:
"When Jesus saw him lying there and knew that he had already been there a long time, he said to him, 'Do you want to be healed?'"

✳ ✳ ✳

There was a certain paralyzed invalid who sat by the pool at Bethsaida for 38 years. Imagine enduring this condition for 38 years! That's longer than many people in that day lived.

He was like many other blind, lame, and paralyzed people gathered around the pool. They believed that if one of God's angels from heaven were to descend to earth and stir the water, whoever entered the pool first would be healed immediately.

Supernaturally, Jesus knew that he'd been sitting by the pool for a very long time—just like he knows all that is occurring in everyone's life. There is nothing hidden from him. He is omniscient over everything in the universe—and what's happening in every person's heart.

Jesus knows what's in your heart today as well. He knows the places where your heart is paralyzed. He knows your hurts, habits, and hangups. You cannot hide them from him. Before you confess your sins to him, he knows of them. His grace and forgiveness are available to you even before you ask for them.

Jesus asked this invalid by the pool a very important question: Do you want to be healed? Sadly, many don't want to be healed—even those who are unhappily hurting. They enjoy wallowing in their weakness. In some cases, it even becomes their identity. They have no problem carelessly meandering down the most dangerous path imaginable:

the path of least resistance. They allow their indolent flesh to rule them—never taking the smallest step toward emotional, spiritual, mental, or physical health.

Is this you? Do you want to be healed? Or are you satisfied in self-pity, mesmerized in mediocrity, ruled by the lusts of your flesh?

If you are ready to be healed inwardly, take one small step toward Jesus. Refuse to remain in your present condition. Speak these words to your heart: "I want to be healed. I want to be made well. Today is my first step toward breaking my addiction, solving this problem, and changing my life's mess. Today, I choose to be well!"

If you make this decision and move toward the Lord, he promises he will be there to meet you. He will walk with you. He will give you the strength and courage you need for the next step. And the next one. And then the next one.

To the faithful, God shows himself faithful. He shows his unfailing love to those who walk in devotion to him. His faithfulness endures as the world he created. The mountains may move or the hills disappear, but God's faithful love will remain.

God is faithful. He can make you well. But remember: It all begins with your desire to be made well. Then you'll be able to take the next steps. These little steps, over time, eventually lead to a long, successful journey.

And you will arrive at his desired destination of physical, mental, spiritual, and emotional health for you.

✳ ✳

The Proof of Faith

Today's Reading: John 5:10-14

HEARING GOD'S VOICE FOR TODAY:
*"Now that day was the Sabbath…Afterward Jesus found
him in the temple and said to him, 'See you are well! Sin
no more, that nothing worse may happen to you.'"*

✳ ✳ ✳

Jesus healed the man who had been lame for 38 years. He healed him
on the Sabbath. In doing so, he shattered the silly traditions of men
that said no healing should happen on the Sabbath. His desire for people to be governed by grace on all days, especially the Sabbath, had
become legalistic imprisonment.

The Sabbath was made for man, not man for the Sabbath. It was
created to give one day's rest that renews minds, bodies, and souls. It
also reconnects spirits with the Lord through worship—the one from
whom all blessings flow. He is the Lord of the Sabbath. He created it.
He knows its purpose. This purpose had been horribly misappropri-
ated by the religious leaders of that day.

His desire is for your heart to be filled with his grace. A personal
relationship with Jesus is not about following rules and regulations—
or the traditions of men. When you know his forgiveness, he lives in
you and you in him. You walk closely and intimately with one another.
You converse throughout the day.

Yet he also doesn't want you to miss this very important truth:
When you know his forgiveness, and you walk closely together, you
are not to forget his moral law. The Ten Commandments are gifts to
you—including the Sabbath. They show you how people should live

in a civil society. They are guardrails on the highway of life designed to keep you from hurt and pain.

Remember that this grace is not earned by obeying the moral law. It is given to you the moment you receive Jesus as Lord and Savior. It's a gift that can never be earned.

And when you've truly received his grace, you will still obey his moral law—not because you have to, but because you want to. Your obedience will please him—the one from whom you've received grace, forgiveness, and eternal life.

That's why Jesus told the healed man to sin no more. When rightly understood, the receiving of his grace and forgiveness should always lead to holy obedience. In response to his indwelling love, his followers live out a righteousness that exceeds the righteousness of those living by the law. There is a desire not to sin.

Joyful are those who desire to obey God's law and search for him with all their hearts. God's law is good, righteous, and holy.

Is there a desire deep within your heart to obey all that the Lord has commanded you to do? Is the greatest desire of your heart obedience to his moral law—the Ten Commandments? Do you yearn to be holy as he is holy? Have you set aside the Sabbath as a day of rest and worship of him?

If yes, it's proof you understand how profound his amazing grace is. It shows you know what he rescued you from so that you don't desire to sin again.

Is this you?

✱ ✱

Audacious Claims

Today's Reading: John 5:15-18

HEARING GOD'S VOICE FOR TODAY:
*"'My Father is working until now, and I am working'... This is
why the Jews were seeking all the more to kill him...he was even
calling God his own Father, making himself equal with God."*

✱ ✱ ✱

The religious leaders were terribly upset with Jesus for healing some-one on the Sabbath. But he told them that his Father is always working for goodness and health—no matter what the day of the week may be. Then he told them that he was doing this same good work that his Father was always doing—no matter what the day of the week.

Their anger raged against him. They knew what he was claiming. And he meant to claim it.

The Father and his Son are mysteriously one. No human can under-stand it. They have forever coexisted in perfect, sovereign love and unity.

Do you see here Jesus' extraordinary claim to deity? Don't miss it. His Father in heaven created the Sabbath, and he is Lord over the Sab-bath—making him and the Father one.

Jesus is exactly like his Father in all attributes. He came to earth to reflect his Father's love to you so you could trust him. He wants you to know his close, bountiful, and sovereign love.

If he had been a mere man, he would have been blaspheming the Father with his words. But he was not. It's the truth. He and the Father are one.

If you have invited Jesus to live in your life, you are one with him as well. Which means you are also one with the Father. That means you have a loving Daddy in heaven eternally connected to your heart. That means God, the Lord of love, is connected to you as well.

Jesus rules over all that is happening to you—today and forever. Nothing that comes to you catches him by surprise. He is the Lord and never changes. He oversees all. And he uses it for your good and his glory.

Please believe today that the Father and the Son dearly love you. They consider you a priceless possession, a valuable treasure.

Trust their love for you today. No matter what you may be experiencing, know that all is working together for good. Don't stop believing for the good to come eventually. It will come. Don't give up. Continue to trust. Cling to faith. Hold fast to Jesus. He is caring for you—even on the Sabbath.

And remember: Your situation is not over until it's good.

That's because your Father in heaven is good.

✳ ✳

Honor Jesus

Today's Reading: John 5:19-24

HEARING GOD'S VOICE FOR TODAY:
"Whoever does not honor the Son does not honor the Father
who sent him…whoever hears my word and believes
him who sent me has eternal life. He does not come
into judgment, but has passed from death to life."

✳ ✳ ✳

God the Father has given to Jesus the right to judge all people. It was his divine pleasure to do so.

Why was this done? He wanted all humans to honor Jesus as they honor him. To honor someone means to prize, value, and esteem him. This is another clear affirmation of Jesus' deity. If someone doesn't honor him, they don't honor the one who sent him.

Jesus is not a mere philosopher, moral teacher, or good man. His true identity includes these options. But he is so much more. He and the Father are one. When you worship Jesus, you worship the Father. When you honor Jesus, you honor the Father.

And whoever believes in Jesus has eternal life—at this very moment. When you've received his forgiveness from your sin, this life is not only a future, eternal assurance. It begins here and now and lasts forever.

From God's perspective, you've already been pronounced not guilty for all your sins. You've already faced the judgment seat. After death, there's no doubt about the destination of your eternal soul. It is already secure in heaven.

Because this is true, there is no reason to fear anything you face. If your eternity is secure in Jesus, why fear anything? What is the worst thing that can happen to you? If you die, you have the joy of spending eternity with him. If death is the worst possible thing that can happen to you, then it ends up being the best thing that can happen because it brings you into his presence.

If your eternity is secure in Jesus, what is there to be anxious about? Do not be afraid of anything. Don't fear, for he is with you. He is your God—closer to you than you can ever imagine. He will comfort you when you are hurting. He will uphold you with his strong right hand when you feel your knees are buckling.

You are the focus of his eternal love and care. Your death has been conquered. Your eternal life is secured. You've already been declared guiltless and adopted into his eternal family. And you will be together forever.

Give your burdens to him. He cares for you. He lifts up all those bent underneath their loads. Trust him, and he will help you.

Live abundantly—beyond all expectations. Be free from all fear and worry. Allow his eternal life and love to fill your heart today, tomorrow, and forever.

As you walk with Jesus, know that he is right by your side. His presence with you is secure—for today and all eternity.

✳ ✳

Total Dependence

Today's Reading: John 5:25-36

HEARING GOD'S VOICE FOR TODAY:
*"I can do nothing on my own. As I hear, I judge, and
my judgment is just, because I seek not my own
will but the will of him who sent me."*

✳ ✳ ✳

Reflect on this truth today: Jesus can do nothing on his own. He is totally dependent on the Father and his strength.

Think about this reality. Jesus was completely connected to his Father and daily needed his strength as he lived on earth. So do you as you are connected to Jesus on a daily basis. Apart from him, you can do nothing. Connected to him, you can do all things.

The Father has given the Son full authority over all humanity. It is Jesus' responsibility to judge all humans. He alone holds the power to give eternal life and death. His judgment is perfect in every way. This is because he seeks first and solely the will of his Father in heaven. He was the one who sent him. He and the Father are one.

God is your source of life. In him, you live and move and have your being. He has guaranteed to you the gift of eternal life.

Today, be still and know that Jesus is your God. He is the one who created you. You are his, the sheep of his pasture. Remain totally in him. Rest completely in him. Don't find your life's meaning or strength in anything or anyone else. From him alone you will find your strength and hope.

Don't seek your own will. Seek first his kingdom. Desire his will— with all your heart, soul, mind, and might. Trust him with all the secondary and tertiary issues in your life.

They are not unimportant to him. He knows your needs. Just seek him first. Your needs will be met.

Listen to the Lord's voice today. He will guide you. Go to where he tells you to go. Feel his promptings to touch another person in your sphere of influence with his love. Go find a hurt and heal it. Go find a need and fill it.

Walk in his grace. Be his hands and feet today. Let his life flow through you to others—as his Father's life flowed through him to you and others who believe in him.

Don't you see? This is Jesus' will for your life each day. He wants you to be an instrument of his healing and peace to the world. He wants you to help him advance his kingdom on earth.

Will you let him lead you? To those who are faithful to what he gives them, he will give even more responsibility.

Through him, you will find the strength to do all things.

That's because nothing is impossible for those who believe in him and are totally connected to him.

Moses Writes About Jesus

Today's Reading: John 5:37-47

HEARING GOD'S VOICE FOR TODAY:
"If you believed Moses, you would believe me, for he wrote of me."

✳ ✳ ✳

The Jews of Jesus' day believed that Moses wrote the Law. From Genesis to Deuteronomy, they trusted that Moses faithfully wrote the words of God. One would assume that if they believed Moses' words, they would have eagerly received Jesus' words—since his words come from the Father as well.

But they did not. Therefore, they must not have believed Moses' words to be from God. Otherwise, they would have believed Jesus' words.

Moses wrote over and over again about Jesus. When he pointed to the coming great prophet, he was referring to Jesus (Deuteronomy 18:15). He is that great prophet. Moses wrote about the high priest alone having access to the Father on behalf of the Jews (Leviticus 8–10). Jesus is that high priest for humanity. Moses wrote about the perfect lamb sacrificed to take away Israel's sins (Leviticus 9:1-10). Jesus is that perfect Lamb of God who takes away the sins of the world. Moses served as the one mediator between God and the children of Israel (Exodus 33:12-15). Jesus is now the one true Mediator who stands between the Father and the sins of humanity.

In one of his resurrection appearances, Jesus walked with two forlorn disciples on the road to Emmaus. During this long walk, he took them through the entire Old Testament and showed them all the passages that pointed to himself—including Moses' writings. Their eyes were opened. Their hearts were strangely stirred. They realized it was Jesus who was walking with them.

Today, please read the Old Testament. It is the Word of God. You will find Jesus all through its pages.

As you read, you will see the Father's plan for salvation unfold over the course of history. He oversaw every single second of Israel's history. He was controlling every event for his purposes. There was an obvious and perfect plan being worked out. This plan finds its fulfillment in Jesus.

If you love Jesus, you are a part of salvation history as well. The Father oversees everything that is happening in your story. Your story is a part of his story.

There is no cosmic chaos. There is omniscient oversight. God is in control. He loves you. He has a perfect plan. You are a part of that plan. He has chosen you to do something only you can do. That's your purpose in life.

Read Jesus' Word every chance you get. It will be a lamp to your feet and a light for your path. It will give you wise counsel. Your eyes will be opened to new instruction.

See Jesus in the pages of the Bible. It all points to him. He is the hero of the Bible.

He wants to be your hero. Let him lead your life.

And you will see your story being lived out in God's greater story.

✳ ✳

The Test of Faith

Today's Reading: John 6:1-13

HEARING GOD'S VOICE FOR TODAY:
"Jesus said to Philip, 'Where are we to buy bread, so
that these people may eat?' He said this to test
him, for he himself knew what he would do."

✳ ✳ ✳

Jesus went away with his followers for some time alone. We all need that. If you don't come apart, you'll come apart. From Jesus' human perspective, it was true for him too.

As Jesus and the disciples tried to rest, the masses figured out where they were. More than 10,000 men, women, and children came. This happened miles away from any place to secure food. Jesus and the disciples knew they'd eventually need to feed the crowd.

That's what prompted Jesus to ask Philip about where to buy food. He was from the area. He was the appropriate person to ask.

But Jesus had an ulterior motive when he asked this question. He already knew the answer. He already knew the solution to the problem. His resources are limitless.

Jesus asked this question to test Philip's faith. It was not yet fully developed. There were lessons he needed to learn.

Yes, Philip had seen Jesus perform multiple miracles. But he still didn't possess a fully orbed faith. That's why he needed to take the test. It was the only way he would realize faith truly existed in his heart.

Jesus does the same with you. It's not because he enjoys placing you in difficult situations. It's because he wants to develop your faith. You may say with your words that you believe in him. But it's only in difficult situations that you can discover if you really trust him.

Teachers know this truth. They give tests to make sure their students know the material. Similarly, Jesus gives his disciples (the word means "pupils") tests to help them grow in their faith. Without faith it is impossible to please him. He loves great faith.

Do you have great faith today? When his tests come to you, do you pass them with flying colors?

Are those words of whining and complaining he hears pouring forth from you during this time of testing? Are you suggesting he doesn't really care for you? Your words show what's in your heart. They mirror a heart of unbelief.

Receive the Lord's tests of faith with great joy—even when they are of the "pop quiz" variety. Though he is silent when giving the tests (as all teachers are), he is administering all of them. They will help mature your heart of faith.

When the test comes, speak to the impossible situation in your life. Tell it to be lifted up and thrown into the heart of the sea. Really believe it. Don't doubt. And see it happen.

His heart's desire is that you pass the test.

That's what's most important to him.

＊＊＊＊＊＊＊＊＊＊＊＊＊＊＊＊＊＊＊＊＊＊＊＊＊＊＊

Who Is Jesus?

Today's Reading: John 6:14-15

HEARING GOD'S VOICE FOR TODAY:
"When the people saw the sign he had done, they said, 'This is indeed the Prophet who is come into the world.' Perceiving then that they were about to come and take him by force to make him king, Jesus withdrew again to the mountain by himself."

＊ ＊ ＊

After Jesus miraculously fed the 10,000-plus people with five loaves and two fish, the crowd concluded he was the Prophet—fulfilling the prophecy of Moses (Deuteronomy 18:15). He perceived they would soon try to force him to be their king.

He withdrew to a private place in the mountain to be alone and pray. He wasn't to be an earthly king. They failed to realize his true identity.

The most important question you can ever ask about him is this: Who is Jesus? Your answer will determine where you spend eternity.

Who is Jesus?

Yes, he is the Prophet about whom Moses prophesied. He spoke truths as a great prophet. Yes, he is a king. He rules over all as a great king does.

But he is so much more. He is the eternal King of kings and Lord of lords. He is God in human flesh, the perfect God/man, conceived in his earthly mother's womb by the miraculous power of the Spirit. He lived perfectly in obedience to the righteous requirements of the Law—something no human can do. He died on the cross as the perfect substitute for your sin. His cross should have been your cross. He died in your place—suffering for a penalty that was yours.

Jesus was raised from the dead, thus proving his deity and confirming the forgiveness of your sins. By grace through faith, you can now receive his gift of eternal life. Just as he was raised from the dead, all those who believe in him will be raised as well.

Who is Jesus?

He is the visible image of the invisible God. He existed before anything else and holds all creation together. He is your way to true life—both eternally and now. He is your closest friend and companion in this life—closer than a brother or sister. He lives in you—the hope of glory. He is daily conforming you to live as he lived—as a servant, not a superstar. The very power and presence of heaven is indwelling you through him—right now.

Listen to his prophetic voice today, guiding you into all truth. Let him rule as a king in your heart, overseeing and controlling everything that comes to you.

Know who Jesus is. Believe in him and you will be saved. Joyfully face your upcoming eternal paradise. Your heart should never be troubled. Believe in the Father. Believe also in Jesus.

As Jesus now sits at the right hand of the Father, know that he will always uphold you with his righteous right hand.

✳ ✳

Don't Be Afraid

Today's Reading: John 6:16-21

HEARING GOD'S VOICE FOR TODAY:
"When they had rowed about three or four miles, they saw Jesus walking on the sea and coming near the boat, and they were frightened. But he said to them, 'It is I; do not be afraid.'"

✳ ✳ ✳

The disciples were crossing the Sea of Galilee. It was approximately six miles to the other side. Jesus was not with them. He watched them from the mountain where he was resting and praying.

The wind blew furiously against them. The sea was rough, yo-yoing their boat up and down, the waves loudly slapping the sides of the boat. They were alone and scared.

They failed to realize this fact: Jesus knew the storm was approaching. He knew what they were going to face before they left the shore. None of this took him by surprise.

As they struggled against the contrary waves, their fear increased. They quickly forgot his miracle with the five loaves and two fish. How quickly people can lose their heart of faith when a storm arises!

As you struggle today against life's wicked winds, blowing contrary to your desires, always remember the facts of this story. Jesus was not surprised by the storm. He took the initiative and came to the disciples. He knew of their struggle. He understood their fears before they felt them.

Jesus is not aloof from your life's storms. He is always moving toward you, knowing what you need from him.

And what does Jesus say to all his fear-filled followers? "It is I; don't be afraid." Fear is the antithesis of faith. Fear destroys faith. Don't be afraid!

And what is the best antidote for fear? It is Jesus' presence. He comes to you, to be with you, in all life's trials and circumstances. He is with you. He upholds you. He strengthens you.

There is nothing, absolutely nothing, that you and Jesus can't face and handle together. His promised presence is what conquers all fear.

Don't be afraid! Take courage. The Lord is with you. Though you may be walking through a dark valley, he is beside you. His spiritual weaponry is available to protect and comfort you. Fasten around yourself his belt of truth. Put on his helmet of salvation. Place his shoes of peace on your feet. Hold high his strong shield of faith to extinguish the fiery darts of the enemy. Know and quote his Word—which is your best offensive weapon against the enemy—along with continuing to pray without ceasing.

Jesus did not give you a spirit of fear, but of love, peace, and a sound mind.

Don't be troubled or afraid. Speak to fear and say, "The Lord is my helper. I will have no fear."

Let Jesus answer the next time fear knocks on the door of your heart. When you do, you'll find fear to be gone.

Seek Jesus

Today's Reading: John 6:22-24

HEARING GOD'S VOICE FOR TODAY:
*"So when the crowd saw that Jesus was not there, nor
his disciples, they themselves got into the boats
and went to Capernaum, seeking Jesus."*

✳ ✳ ✳

After Jesus had fed the 10,000-plus people, word about the miracle
spread quickly. Throngs tried to find out where he was staying.
When they couldn't find him, they continued seeking him.

Why do you seek him? This crowd simply wanted more food. They
just wanted another miracle. They wanted Jesus to serve them. They
didn't desire to serve him. They sought a magic genie in a bottle—a
genie that would say to them, "Your wish is my command."

That's not the kind of follower Jesus desires. When someone seeks
him and chooses to follow him, they need to know they are choosing to deny themselves, take up their cross, and follow him. They are
choosing to die to self and live for his glory. They are choosing to crucify their own lusts of the flesh and live a holy life that emulates who he
is. They are choosing to leave any other god, lust, or passion that would
be placed above him. They are choosing to seek first his kingdom and
his way of right living.

It's a life that demands your soul, effort, and energy—your all.

Why do you seek Jesus?

If you are truly seeking him, you will find him. True spiritual seekers will always discover him and choose to live for him. He is their first
priority. They choose serving over being a celebrity. Any praise they

receive is like a rose that is smelled and enjoyed, but then given to him. They know every gift they have comes from him.

Why do you seek Jesus? Be honest with your answer. Are you following him for him to serve you, or for you to serve him? For your glory or his?

Know that as you follow him, he promises to meet your every need. He is concerned with every area of your life. He wants you to enjoy life and to do so abundantly. He is not a miser. He doesn't withhold blessings from his followers who do what is right. He loves to give blessings to those who trust him and make the Lord their confidence and hope. He enjoys giving his favor generously to people who need and desire him.

Jesus is good and kind. His mercies endure forever. He is worthy to be followed.

Just make sure you know why you are seeking him. And what it will cost you to follow him.

It's very important that you rightly know. When you do, you will be able to persevere until the end.

The Work of Faith

Today's Reading: John 6:25-34

HEARING GOD'S VOICE FOR TODAY:
"Jesus answered him, 'This is the work of God, that
you believe in him whom he has sent.'"

※ ※ ※

Jesus had just told his listeners that they should not labor for food that doesn't last. Their life's focus should not be on things that are temporary and have no eternal value. Their eyes should be fixed on heaven, not on the things of this world.

But they completely misunderstood what he was saying. They wanted him to show them certain works that they could do so they could possess eternal life. That's called self-righteousness. Humans desire to know and obey laws that make them righteous in the Father's eyes.

Jesus told them this eternal truth: The one work that the Father requires for people to be declared righteous is to believe in him. You are to believe that he died on the cross for the forgiveness of your sin. The one work required to enter heaven is to trust in his completed work on the cross. That's all that is needed.

But your faith in the cross is a very hard work to do. Why? You have never seen Jesus, yet you are still called to believe in him. Faith is the assurance of things hoped for, the conviction of things *not* seen. Without faith, it is tacitly impossible to please him.

This kind of faith is especially challenging when life makes no sense. It's very difficult to continue to believe in the Lord when pain increases and you can't see your next step. It's hard when you feel betrayed, unloved, and deserted and you want to give up on life. It's hard to believe when life gets challenging.

But that's what Jesus calls you to do. He asks you to follow him by faith, not sight. He asks you to love him though you've never seen him. He asks you to trust that he is with you always, even when the next step cannot be seen.

Real faith demands you lean on him in complete dependence no matter what. It believes he will lift you out of the pit of despair.

Jesus loves great faith. It pleases him when you believe he can do the impossible. He loves when you trust him in everything that's happening—especially when it's difficult.

Jesus knows you face some days when you feel as if you are drowning. He realizes there are times when you want to give up. When that happens, trust him. Fight the fight of faith. He will help you to keep moving forward. His power works best in your weakness. Be strong and courageous. Don't be afraid or discouraged. He will be with you wherever you go.

Yes, it's a very broken world in which you live. Jesus suffered in it as well. But rejoice! He has overcome the world. He is your strength and shield. Yield your life to him alone. Let him be your life's desire. Believe that the more you suffer, the more he showers his comfort on you. Choose to worship him in the tough times.

Work hard to believe in him, even when it's difficult to do so.

It's the only work necessary to inherit eternal life.

✳ ✳

Jesus Is the Bread of Life

Today's Reading: John 6:35-40

HEARING GOD'S VOICE FOR TODAY:
"Jesus said to them, 'I am the bread of life; whoever comes to me shall not hunger, and whoever believes in me shall never thirst.'"

✳ ✳ ✳

Every faithful Jew would know the significance of Jesus' "I am" statements. When Moses was called by God to deliver the Israelites from the bondage of Egyptian slavery, he asked God to give him his name so he could tell the Egyptians who was sending him. God responded, "I AM WHO I AM." It was God's holy name that all Jews sacredly honored for centuries. It was considered so holy that faithful Jews didn't think it should be uttered.

When Jesus used the "I am" phrase, it was a clear reference to his identity. More specifically, when he said, "I am the bread of life," he was saying that he alone is the one who can fill the hunger of the human heart.

Jesus nourishes people spiritually. When literal bread is eaten, eventually your hunger returns. But when you ingest Jesus and invite him to live in and with you, he offers a spiritual sustenance that satisfies your soul forever. You will never hunger again. You are eternally satisfied when you hunger and thirst for righteousness.

How do you receive this spiritual food? By believing in him. Believe he is who he says he is. What are your options? Was he a liar? That's impossible. He is perfect truth. Was he crazy? There is nothing crazy about anything Jesus teaches. His words give sanity to the despairing.

If Jesus is not lying or crazy, what other option is there? He is who he says he is. He is the bread of life. He is God in human flesh. If you partake of his life in you, you are forever satisfied. Your soul will be nourished forever.

God's Word is true. It gives wise advice for everyday living. It should comfort you. It gives light so that even the simple can understand it. It is more desirable than fine gold, even the finest gold. It is sweeter than honey, even honey dripping from the comb. It warns us of potential danger. There is great reward for those who obey it.

Don't live solely by the bread of this world. It is transient. It won't last. Rather, live by every word that proceeds from the Lord's mouth.

Then you'll experience life as he intended it to be lived. You will know the depth, width, and height of his grace for you. You will experience his inexpressible joy inside your heart. His peace that passes all understanding will be yours. The pressures of life will be moderated. His kindness will consume you. Your decisions that you make throughout the day will be his decisions.

Feast upon Jesus today.

He is your personal bread of life—today and forever.

Stop Grumbling

Today's Reading: John 6:41-51

HEARING GOD'S VOICE FOR TODAY:
*"Jesus answered them, 'Do not grumble among yourselves.
No one can come to me unless the Father who sent me
draws him. And I will raise him up on the last day.'"*

✳ ✳ ✳

The Jews grumbled because Jesus had said he was the bread that came down from heaven. They even hinted at the rumors of his purported illegitimate birth. It's a classic strategy of debate. If you don't like the argument, attack the person making the argument.

Be careful about grumbling. It caused the Israelites to wander in the wilderness for 40 years. It's unbelief. It shows you don't trust the Lord. It's sin. If you complain, you remain in the wilderness. Do not grumble among yourselves—ever! Rather, believe. Trust Jesus in every facet of your life. The opposite of grumbling is trust.

And remember this truth: Anyone who believes in the Son does so solely because the Father in heaven draws him. That was why he sent Jesus.

There is nothing meritorious within you to earn Jesus' favor. You were dead in your sins and trespasses. That means only a divine power outside of you can give you life. Before you chose Jesus, the Spirit was working on your heart to make you alive in him.

Why is this important? It means God alone receives the praise and glory. It makes him alone the one worthy of all honor, dominion, and power. He alone is the author and finisher of your faith. He alone demands all our life, soul, mind, and energy. In light of all that, he alone is worthy of your worship.

How does the Father's perfect sovereignty and your will work together for your eternal salvation? Some people see these two truths as contradictory. But they are not. They are like two train tracks that run parallel with one another until they ostensibly come together on the distant horizon. They seem disparate here. But they do come together in the future. We may not understand this now, but we will in eternity.

Heavenly mysteries belong to God alone. Don't let your puny, finite mind dwell on things too difficult and majestic for you to understand.

One day you will comprehend doctrinal difficulties. Questions that puzzled you will be answered. Now you look through a mirror dimly. Later, you will see the Lord face-to-face. And he will explain all to you.

That's why the most-often-spoken word in heaven will be "Oh!" As Jesus explains to you all that you didn't understand, your eternal eyes will widen with amazement as you grasp why he was doing what he did in your life. "Oh! Oh! Oh!" you will continually exclaim.

There is eternal purpose in everything. God has reasons for all that he allows to happen in your life. In eternity, it will all make sense to you.

Until then, continue to trust him. He drew you to the Father. He will raise you up on the last day.

✳ ✳

Ingesting Eternal Life

Today's Reading: John 6:52-59

HEARING GOD'S VOICE FOR TODAY:
"The Jews then disputed among themselves, saying, 'How can this man give us his flesh to eat?' So Jesus said to them, 'Truly, truly I say to you, unless you eat the flesh of the Son of Man and drink his blood, you have no life in you. Whoever feeds on my flesh and drinks my blood has eternal life, and I will raise him up on the last day.'"

✳ ✳ ✳

Is this teaching difficult for you to understand? Here, Jesus is teaching deep, internal, and eternal truths using a human illustration. So don't take this literally.

What was he teaching? To "eat my flesh" and "drink my blood" means to ingest him totally in your life. It means trusting him completely—especially when it comes to his death on the cross and the forgiveness of your sins. You need to ingest and digest the reality of his grace, mercy, and kindness living in you every day. You need to chew on it like a cow does its cud, letting his grace and mercy nourish you throughout the day.

This truth is also expressed at the communion table the Lord gave to you. Whenever you receive the bread and wine, representing Jesus' flesh and blood, you are reminded of and experience anew his spiritual presence in your life. You remember the meaning and significance of the cross. You know the Lord is compassionate and merciful, slow to anger, and filled with unfailing grace. Your faith in him is renewed. Your life in him is mysteriously recharged.

You know you have eternal life. You know you will be raised up on the last day. There should be no doubt in your mind. It's an absolute certainty. Death has lost its sting. The grave has been conquered.

This is pure, profound, and prolific unconditional love. It's not that you first loved him, but that he first loved you. Before the foundations of the earth were ever formed, he first loved you. His love for you began before this world was ever made.

Jesus gave up his life as an atoning sacrifice for your sins. He took upon himself the punishment you deserved so he could give you the gift of eternal life. He went through the agony of his suffering so his grace could consume your heart.

Eat of his flesh. Drink of his blood. Be totally consumed with his grace. It's inexhaustible.

Jesus is eager to relent and not punish. He loves to repay two blessings for each of your troubles. He loves you so very much!

This love is patient and kind. It doesn't envy or boast. It isn't arrogant or rude. It doesn't need to be right. It isn't irritable or resentful. It doesn't rejoice with evil, but celebrates the truth. This love bears all things, believes all things, hopes all things, and endures all things. It never fails.

Nor will this love fail you today. It will be profusely powerful in your heart no matter what you may face. This love that sustains you today will one day carry you into Jesus' presence.

Feed on this truth.

And you will be filled with the joy of his presence.

The Words of Eternal Life

Today's Reading: John 6:60-71

HEARING GOD'S VOICE FOR TODAY:

"After this many of his disciples turned back and no longer walked with him. So Jesus said to the Twelve, 'Do you want to go as well?' Simon Peter answered him, 'Lord, to whom shall we go? You have the words of eternal life, and we have believed, and have come to know that you are the Holy One of God.'"

✳ ✳ ✳

Many followed Jesus after he had fed them. But when he talked about eating his flesh and drinking his blood—being totally committed to him until death—the masses melted away. They followed him only as long as he met their needs.

Don't misunderstand. He is concerned for your daily needs. You are to pray to the Father to give you your daily bread.

But following Jesus is not about him benefiting you. It's about your willingness to do what he says no matter what the cost. The crowds weren't willing to pay this price.

Is this you? Do you follow the Lord only for what he will give to you? Or do you follow him because you know that he alone holds the keys for a meaningful life? As he died for you, are you willing to die for him? That's the cost of discipleship.

After the masses had left, Jesus asked the Twelve if they were going to leave him as well. Simon Peter answered correctly. He realized that only Jesus had the words of eternal life. He recognized Jesus was the Holy One of God. He realized there was no other person who held this truth. Peter had believed in him. His faith was settled.

Is your faith settled? Is there any room for doubt? There should not be. Your doubt will cause your faith to be tossed to and fro—like the tide erasing a truth you just etched in the sand. It forces a divided loyalty. That's why your faith should not waver.

How will you know if you truly are one of Jesus' disciples? You will be one of his disciples tomorrow. And the day after that. And the day after that. Your perseverance in faith until the end of your life proves you are one of his faithful followers.

Yes, you will still have much to learn about following Jesus. That's okay. The Twelve had much to learn as well. Just keep learning. Keep obeying what he says—even if you don't understand why. He has his reasons. Sometimes they are hidden in heaven. But there are reasons behind his principles. Trust and obey them—and him. Every time you do, your faith grows stronger.

He alone holds the words of eternal life. No one else does. Every other teaching pales in comparison to his.

Jesus is the Holy One, sent from his Father in heaven because of his great love for you. He is working in you, giving you the desire and the power to do what pleases him. Your eternity is in his hands.

Trust him today in everything that happens to you.

And remember this truth: Only Jesus holds the words to eternal life.

✳ ✳

Being a Servant

Today's Reading: John 7:1-9

Hearing God's Voice for Today:

"Now the Feast of Booths was at hand. So his brothers said to him, 'Leave here and go to Judea, that your disciples also may see the works you are doing. For no one works in secret if he seeks to be known openly. If you do these things, show yourself to the world.' For not even his brothers believed in him. Jesus said to them, 'My time has not yet come, your time is always here.'"

✳ ✳ ✳

Jesus had earthly brothers and sisters. He was the firstborn in his family. His brothers and sisters grew up with him. They knew him. But they did not understand his mission on earth and why his Father sent him here.

The Feast of Booths in Jerusalem was a time of year when thousands of faithful Jews would come to Jerusalem to celebrate God's faithfulness while they were wandering in the wilderness. Jesus' brothers saw this time as an opportunity to increase his popularity and gain an even larger following. "You need a brand, a platform, to increase your followers," they were saying.

That's how the world thinks. It wants celebrities. But Jesus came to serve. His path is one of a suffering servant. His way to change the world is not through you being a celebrity, but a servant. It's when you are humble that the Father lifts you up.

Jesus steadfastly refused to think in the way his brothers did. That's why he said, "My time has not yet come." He would not be manipulated by their worldly thinking. He reminded them that the time to die on the cross had not yet arrived. That time was solely in the hands of his Father in heaven. It was not yet the Father's will for him to publicly go to Jerusalem.

Please understand this truth: When you give your life to Jesus, everything is under the sovereign timing of the Father. There is a time, season, and purpose for everything under the sun. God is the unseen Seer. He oversees all. Nothing is beyond his control—especially your life.

Are you waiting patiently for something today? Is there a promise you feel you've received from the Father that hasn't yet happened? Don't give up. Continue to wait patiently for the answer at God's appointed time. Strength arises within you when you wait on the Father's perfect timing.

As you wait, feel the Father lift you up like the wind under an eagle's wings. Feel him lifting you higher and higher—to the heavens before his throne. You will run and not become weary. You will walk and not faint.

Don't give up your dreams. Keep persevering. If the Father has given it to you, he cannot lie. Therefore, your dreams cannot die.

There is purpose in the waiting. There is a plan. There is a time and season for your promise to be fulfilled.

Wait patiently in faith.

Your answer could be just a short time away!

Choose to Obey God's Will

Today's Reading: John 7:10-24

HEARING GOD'S VOICE FOR TODAY:
"If anyone's will is to do God's will, he will know whether the teaching is from God or whether I am speaking on my own authority. The one who speaks on his own authority seeks his own glory; but the one who seeks the glory of him who sent him is true, and in him there is no falsehood."

✳ ✳ ✳

If your will is to absolutely do the Father's will, you will know who Jesus is. You will know that his teachings are true. You will know that he doesn't speak on his own authority, but by the authority of the one who sent him.

Or do you seek your own glory in life? Do you speak with your own authoritative opinions—ones ensnarled in nothing but your own perspectives? If so, you will never know that Jesus is the way, the truth, and the life. You will never know the glory of the Father revealed in him.

The Father alone is worthy of all praise. Through him alone you live and move and have your being. He will not share his glory with any frail, fallen, and feeble human being.

If you believe in Jesus, you will desire to obey him. If you love him, you will obey his commandments. In your head and heart, you will know that he is God's Son who came to forgive the sins of the world—and your personal sins. Obedience to his teachings will be the proof of your love for and commitment to him.

Obey the Lord today. Joyful are those who obey his laws and search for him with all their hearts. But also remember: All your life choices greatly affect who you are and the person you will become.

Why do you make certain choices? Are they motivated by your feelings? Or by your circumstances? These things are fleeting and transitory. They change by the moment. If your feelings or circumstances determine your choices, you are most likely seeking your own glory and not the Father's.

Or is culture influencing your decisions? Don't rely on it. It is always changing as well. It shifts with the whims and fancies of the masses. It's nuanced by negativism. It's driven by the cult of personality. It focuses on self-fulfillment.

Rather, trust the immutable Father of the universe. He never changes. Obey based on who Jesus is and what he says. His authority comes from heaven. What he commands you to do is rooted in the changeless principles of a changeless God.

When you obey Jesus' commands, you are doing his will. It proves you believe he is the truth. It proves you love him. It shows you have wholeheartedly made him Lord of your life.

Follow all that Jesus teaches you. When you do, it proves you belong to him.

It also gives the Father in heaven all the honor, glory, and praise—from this day forth and for all eternity.

Glorify him. Enjoy him forever.

This is your chief reason for living.

✳ ✳

Jesus Knows the Father

Today's Reading: John 7:25-31

HEARING GOD'S VOICE FOR TODAY:
"So Jesus proclaimed, as he taught in the temple, 'You know me, and you know where I come from. But I have not come of my own accord. He who sent me is true, and him you do not know. I know him, for I come from him, and he sent me.'"

✳ ✳ ✳

People often assume they know more about Jesus than they do. They've never taken the time to explore what he has actually claimed. Subsequently, they make wild, audacious statements about him that are far from true.

As Jesus taught in the Temple, some Jews did the same thing. They thought they knew his identity—especially the specifics about where he was from. They concluded the Messiah could not have Jesus' background.

They failed to realize Jesus' true home. He was sent from heaven. He didn't come on his own accord. He was asked by his Father to leave the splendor of heaven and come to the squalor of this world.

Do you know why Jesus was sent? He became a baby in a manger to live the righteous life you can't live because of your sin. He was sent to die a hideous death you should have died. He took your shame upon himself and gave you his righteousness—all a gift by grace through faith—rooted in the Father's love for you.

Jesus knows the Father. He came from him. The Father alone sent the Son.

And Jesus gladly obeyed—so that you could be forgiven of your sins and have an intimate, personal, and dynamic relationship with him forever. It was for love—for you—that he came.

Do you know the extent of Jesus' abiding love for you? If you feel any condemnation, it's not from him. How could he die for you and then condemn you? How could he justify you, declaring you not guilty before the Father, and make accusation against you? How could he offer incessant intercession for you and prosecute you at the same time? It's implausible and makes no sense.

If you feel condemnation, it's from the enemy. He is the accuser of those who believe in Jesus. He wants to paralyze you with guilt. He desires to put you on the sidelines of life with a spiritual ACL injury. He hopes to paralyze your Christian walk.

There is no condemnation for those who know Jesus' love. None. Don't listen to those voices of accusation in your mind. They are not from Jesus. He is for you—on your side!

No shadow of shame ever darkens the face of God's people. Those who look to him are free from guilt and are radiant with joy. God forgives wickedness and never again remembers sin.

God loves you. You are his. Nothing can ever separate you from his love. It is secure.

He said so.

And God speaks nothing but the truth.

✳ ✳

Your Eternal Home

Today's Reading: John 7:32-36

HEARING GOD'S VOICE FOR TODAY:
"Jesus then said, 'I will be with you a little longer, and
then I am going to him who sent me. You will see me, and
you will not find me. Where I am you cannot come.'"

✳ ✳ ✳

There is an old saying: "If you don't like the message, kill the messenger." That was the position of the chief priests and Pharisees—those who represented the ruling body of the Jews, called the Sanhedrin. After hearing Jesus' teachings, they desired to arrest and kill him.

Jesus knew what would happen next. The Temple guard would attempt to arrest him. But they would not find him. His time to be arrested and die on the cross had not yet come.

When Jesus said, "Where I am you cannot come," he was alluding to his future ascension. After his death and resurrection, he would return to his Father in heaven. He would sit at the Father's right hand—having been given all power and authority to rule over the universe. From this position of power, Jesus will one day return to judge the living and the dead. He will give eternal life to some, and eternal condemnation to others.

Jesus was saying that when he ascended to heaven, he was going to a place where the chief priests couldn't follow him. They didn't believe in him. They wanted to kill him! How could people who wanted to kill him inherit the gift of eternal life? They couldn't.

If you believe in Jesus, you have eternal life. It's a free gift guaranteed to you—by grace through faith alone. Good works cannot earn this gift. You can never do enough good works to please the Father. That's why Jesus needed to take the excruciating punishment of your sins upon himself and give you his righteousness.

Some call this "the great exchange." You received the much better end of the deal. Jesus received your guilt, blame, shame, and punishment. You then received his forgiveness, grace, mercy, and kindness. He never remembers your sin. You also get to go to heaven. All this is given to you as a free gift. It is undeserved and unmerited.

Why would Jesus do this for you? Because of his love for you, and because he wants you to live in the power of his grace. When you receive his unconditional love, your life is forever changed. You start desiring to live how he wants you to live. Your life starts to reflect Jesus' in and through you. You begin to be conformed to his image.

Live in that love today. Be consumed by his unconditional grace. Grab hold of it tenaciously. Make his grace your heart's lifeline.

And know the truth that if you believe in him, you will go to the place where he is. Heaven will be your home.

If it weren't so, Jesus wouldn't have promised it to you.

✳ ✳

Living Water

Today's Reading: John 7:37-39

HEARING GOD'S VOICE FOR TODAY:
*"Jesus stood up and cried out, 'If anyone thirsts, let him
come to me and drink. Whoever believes in me, as the
Scripture has said, "Out of his heart will flow rivers of living
water."' Now this he said about the Spirit, whom those
who believed in him were to receive, for as yet the Spirit
had not been given, because Jesus was not yet glorified."*

✳ ✳ ✳

J esus is the source of all life, and he is the one who continues to give
you a meaningful life.

Once he has placed his Spirit in you, you will never thirst again.
Anyone who believes in him receives the gift of his inward presence
through the Spirit. When you come and drink from him, he will forever satisfy every one of your longings.

This belief is not mere intellectual assent. Rather, it is an inextric-
able, life-giving, eternal reality—an eternal connection between you
and Jesus. He lives in you. You live in him. He is your source of life
and hope. Daily, you drink from him and his grace, love, mercy, and
kindness. Whatever is happening to you, you first come to him and
drink from his life. And he will satisfy the deepest longings of your
eternal soul.

That's why you need a daily time with him. It is essential for your
health.

The living water from which you drink is inexhaustible. It flows
from deep within your heart. Please note it "flows." It's not a trickle or

a little stream. It gushes forth with grace. It's a flood of God's favor. It's living water—not stagnant or brackish. It is pure, fresh, and flowing. No germs or parasites can live in it. When you drink of it, you receive abundant life.

If you feel heavy-laden by any burdens today, give them all to Jesus—all of them. Drink from him. Don't continue to hold on to even one problem or concern.

Make sure you are connected to the Spirit, who lives in you. He is your life source—living deep inside you. He connects you to Jesus. As you remain in him, fruitfulness flows from your life. Your character is changed. God's righteousness is evident. Your transformed life glorifies the Father in heaven.

Let the Spirit's inward water give life to your dry soul. Let him bring comfort when you face discouragement. Have hope in your heart. He promises his presence.

Then his love will replace apathy. Forgiveness will replace bitterness. Patience will replace anger. Kindness will replace criticism. Gentleness will replace pride. Joy will replace discouragement. Courage will replace timidity. Faith will replace fear. Hope will replace despair. Peace will replace anxiety. Self-control will replace self-indulgence. Collaboration will replace strife. Your focus will be on others, not yourself.

And the Lord's streams of living water will forever flow in you. He will give you moral excellence, which will lead to knowledge. This knowledge will produce self-control, which will lead to patient endurance. This patient endurance gives godliness, and godliness leads to brotherly affection. And brotherly affection produces love for everyone.

Jesus' living water produces all these wonderful qualities. And he is calling you to give his living water to a dying, parched world that desperately needs it.

That's one of the key reasons the Lord created you.

No One Has Ever Taught Like Jesus

Today's Reading: John 7:40-52

HEARING GOD'S VOICE FOR TODAY:
"The officers then came to the chief priests and Pharisees,
who said to them, 'Why did you not bring him?' The
officers answered, 'No one ever spoke like this man.'"

✳ ✳ ✳

The Temple police had been deployed by the chief priests and Pharisees to arrest Jesus. Upon their return, they were questioned why they had not arrested him.

Their response is telling and profound: "No one ever spoke like this man!"

What they said was true. No human had ever taught like Jesus did. They can't. No other person in history has been fully divine and fully human at the same time. Because Jesus was divine, when he spoke, he did so with the authority of his Father in heaven. He was giving insights from him. He spoke with perfect truth and wisdom.

That was what the officers heard. That's why they were confounded and couldn't arrest him. His teachings pointed to his true identity. Deep inside, they knew they couldn't arrest God in human flesh.

As you take time to carefully read Jesus' teachings, they will become indelibly etched in your soul. You will sense God's authority speaking to you. You will experience his goodness. Similarly, you will feel your total depravity—how much you've hurt God's heart. Recognize the cry of your soul: "I need a Savior." Jesus is that Savior.

See yourself as a lost sheep who has wandered away from the rest of the herd. Yet you are still precious to Jesus. He would have left heaven and died for you even if you were the only person on earth.

See yourself as the rebellious son wallowing in a pigsty. You've made a mess of your life. See yourself as being awakened to your hideous condition and wanting to go home. See yourself as one being welcomed home by an unconditionally loving Father in heaven—with a smile on his face and his arms opened wide toward you.

See yourself as the pearl of great price being purchased by a merchant no matter what the cost. You are that pearl. See yourself as a hidden treasure covered in a field. Jesus has found you. Now he gives everything, even his life, to own you. Jesus was willing to go to any extreme to purchase your freedom from sin. In fact, he died on a cross to own you! That's the extent of his love for you.

Jesus' love for you could not be greater. He rescued you from the kingdom of darkness and transferred you into his kingdom of light. He purchased your freedom and forgave your sins. You now stand before him blameless, without a single fault. His teachings should overwhelm your heart with how much he cares for you.

No one has ever taught like Jesus.

That's because there has never been one like Jesus.

✳ ✳

Realize Your Sinfulness

Today's Reading: John 8:1-11

HEARING GOD'S VOICE FOR TODAY:
"He stood up and said to them, 'Let him who is without sin among you be the first to throw a stone at her.' And even more he bent down and wrote on the ground. But when they heard it, they went away one by one, beginning with the older ones, and Jesus was left alone with the woman standing before him."

✳ ✳ ✳

A woman had been caught in the act of adultery. The religious leaders badgered Jesus to have her stoned to death in accordance with the Law of Moses. They tried relentlessly to entrap him. If he had agreed she should be stoned to death, he would have been accused of having a hard heart and no compassion. If he hadn't agreed, they would have accused him of not obeying the Law of Moses.

In anger and arrogance, the crowd clutched their stones. Jesus' slightest nod of approval would have triggered the first stone to be hurled. His response was different than anticipated. He asked for the person who had never sinned to throw the first stone.

Then Jesus continued to write in the sand. What did he write? Some believe he scribbled down the sins of those ready to jettison rocks—their lack of compassion, their hypocrisy, pride, arrogance, and self-righteousness. Perhaps he wrote the name of the woman—whose life he lovingly clutched in his hands.

Then the Holy Spirit began to prick the hearts of those in the crowd. Slowly but surely, he convicted them of their own sins. As the defenseless woman quivered in fear, each person began dropping the stones they were clutching—beginning with the oldest.

This is how it should be. All have sinned and fallen short of God's glory. But the older a person becomes, the more aware he is of his wicked, selfish, and deceitful heart. The longer people live, the more opportunities they've had to realize their selfish motives and actions.

People love Jesus in direct proportion to how great a sinner they know themselves to be. If you don't think you've sinned much, you won't love him much. But if you know you are a great sinner, you will love him greatly.

Today, open your heart wide to the convictions of the Holy Spirit. Let him prick your heart of your pride. Let him make you aware of your arrogance. Let him confront your lack of compassion. Let him expose your hypocrisy. Let him reveal how far you have fallen short of the Father's perfect will for your life.

Blessed are the poor in spirit. They alone know God's kingdom. Blessed are those who mourn over the sinful condition of their soul. They alone receive the comfort of his forgiveness and grace. Blessed are the broken. They alone know the fullness of his love.

Are you broken today? Have you come to grips with your rebellion against God?

If so, you are ready to drop your stones of self-righteousness and receive Jesus' full forgiveness, grace, mercy, love, and kindness. Your guilt is gone. You are made right with God. His love lives inside you.

You will go and sin no more. You will love the Lord more than you love your sin.

Realizing your sinfulness is the necessary first step in your relationship with him.

✳ ✳

Jesus Is Your Light

Today's Reading: John 8:12-20

HEARING GOD'S VOICE FOR TODAY:
"Jesus spoke to them, saying, 'I am the light of the world. Whoever follows me will not walk in darkness, but will have the light of life.'"

✳ ✳ ✳

Here is the second of Jesus' "I am" statements in John's Gospel. He is sharing his true identity—God in human flesh, sent from heaven as the light of salvation. He came to give light to all human darkness.

Jesus shines his light into the darkness of your soul, revealing how dark it truly is. This light also reveals the steps to escaping your darkened condition and moving into the light. He shows you the answers to the questions that haunt your heart.

You wonder if there is life after this one? Jesus shines his light toward heaven's gates to show you your way home. You wonder if that wound left in darkness will ever heal? He shines his light into your hurting heart to begin your healing. You wonder if there's any future for you? He shines his light into your despairing heart to give you hope. You wonder if it's safe to keep moving forward in life? He shines his light on your life's path so you will know the next step you should take.

Jesus is the light of the world. More importantly, he is *your* light in the world. When you know him and trust him with every area of your life, you have the source of all light living inside you.

His light is stronger than any darkness. Light a single match in a dark room, and it overpowers the darkness. Likewise, all darkness must flee before the overpowering strength of Jesus' light—no matter how small it may be.

The sun, moon, and stars prove this reality. They overcome all darkness. And the brighter the light, the less darkness there is. Think about the sun at high noon on a cloudless day. There is no darkness. There is only clarity.

But think about this reality as well: In heaven there will be no need for a sun, moon, or stars. Jesus' very presence will light up the New Jerusalem and all of heaven. His light will dominate every part of the new heaven and new earth.

He is the light of all other lights. He is the light of the world. He is your light today as you walk in this world. He is a lamp to your feet, showing you your next step as you move toward your eternal destiny.

Believe in Jesus today. Trust him with your next step. Believe what he says about himself. Call on him in your time of trouble. He wants to rescue you.

Jesus has not forgotten about you. He helps the fallen and lifts them up beneath their loads. Though you may trip, you will never fall. He holds you by your hand and listens to your cries for help. He is the strength of your heart. You belong to him. He is yours forever. He is your light.

In him, all your places of darkness can be overcome.

He is stronger than any dark place in your life.

✳ ✳

Desire God's Will

Today's Reading: John 8:21-30

HEARING GOD'S VOICE FOR TODAY:
*"Jesus said to them, 'When you have lifted up the Son of Man,
then you will know that I am he, and that I do nothing
on my own authority, but speak just as the Father taught
me. And he who sent me is with me. He has not left me
alone, for I always do the things that are pleasing to him.'
As he was saying these things, man believed in him."*

✳ ✳ ✳

This teaching from Jesus is of great importance. Many listeners at the time didn't understand what he said because they were earthly minded. But when they "lifted up the Son of Man," when they crucified him, some came to realize who he was—the Son of the Living God and the Lamb of God who takes away all the world's sins.

When they saw the cross, the Holy Spirit revealed Jesus' identity to them. They came to believe in him. And they trusted him with their lives and eternity.

Jesus did nothing on his own authority. He purposefully chose to leave his equality with the Father when he put on human flesh and died on a cross for the forgiveness of your sins. While on earth, he spoke only what the Father said to him. The Father and the Son are inextricably and eternally connected. They are of the same nature and mind. They are one.

Because of the Father's abiding presence in Jesus, he wanted only what was pleasing to him. His will was to do the Father's will alone— to perfectly obey all that the Father commanded him to do. He did. All his good works were in obedience to the Father's will—including his death on the cross. Everything Jesus did was meant to glorify the Father.

Do you believe in Jesus? Do you love him? If so, there is one thing that proves you do. As you are unquestioningly connected to him, the Father's authority will reign over you as it did in Jesus. As the Son intentionally lived to do the Father's will, so will you live to seek first his kingdom and to do his will.

All authority in heaven and on earth has been granted to Jesus. That means that as he lives in you, he will speak to you and guide your life. He will share with you how you are to obey him every day.

Your greatest desire will then become the doing of the Father's will in your life—in the same way as Jesus desired only to do his Father's will. As he was under the Father's authority, so you are under the Son's authority.

Please do whatever Jesus tells you to do. Perform all the good works that you know he desires for you to do. Labor enthusiastically for him. Nothing you do for him is useless. Remember that the Lord will reward each person for the good he does.

When you do these good works, you will bring glory to him. People who do not love Jesus will respect the way you live and be drawn toward your Father in heaven. The way you live can help render a good opinion of him. Living so that the Lord is glorified should be your life's aim in everything you do.

Believe in Jesus. Be totally yielded to his authority over your life. Make the doing of his will your master passion.

When you do, you will prove your love for him.

✳✳✳✳✳✳✳✳✳✳✳✳✳✳✳✳✳✳✳✳✳✳✳✳✳✳✳✳✳✳✳✳

You Are Free!

Today's Reading: John 8:31-38

HEARING GOD'S VOICE FOR TODAY:

*"Jesus said to the Jews who had believed in him, 'If you abide in
my words, you are truly my disciples, and you will know the truth,
and the truth will set you free...Everyone who commits sin is a
slave to sin. The slave does not remain in the house forever; the son
remains forever. So if the Son sets you free, you will be free indeed.'"*

✳ ✳ ✳

Jesus didn't call people to merely make decisions about him. He called
them to be his disciples. A decision is merely a starting point. A disciple is one who is constantly learning from him.

A true disciple is one who abides in the Lord's words. To abide
means to let his life continually live in and through you. You are his disciple when you walk with him daily. There is a continual conversation
between you two. There is a developing trust in and obedience to him.

One major benefit of abiding in Jesus' word is that you will know
the truth. As he indwells you, he will guide you into all truth.

And when you know his truth, you will be set free. This is a promise for all his disciples.

Jesus came to earth to set all captives free from the power of sin and
death. He wants to remove all the chains that hinder you from being
the person he intended you to be. He came to give you abundant life,
not imprisonment. Everyone who commits sin is a slave to sin. Whenever you give in to sin, you increasingly become a slave to that sin. You
can't enjoy life as Jesus intended when you are enslaved to sin.

How does he set you free? By giving you a new identity. You are adopted into his family. You are no longer a slave, but a son or daughter of the King of the universe. A slave cannot live permanently in the master's house. After working in the house, he must leave and return to his slave quarters. A slave also finds his identity solely in the chores he does daily for the master.

It's different with you! When you come to Jesus, you are not only forgiven, but also adopted into his family. You become a permanent member of and resident in the Father's house. You are forever a part of his family. You share his name. You're an heir of all he owns. There are no fears of expulsion from his house—ever!

In addition, your identity is no longer defined by what you do, but by who you are because of your adoption. You don't live in fear of the master's punishment. Your spirit now hears daily from the Holy Spirit that you are an adopted, beloved child of the King of kings. You are free from all condemnation.

Please learn this truth: To be free from sin, you must love something more than the sin. When you know the Father's love, you know your new identity as a son or daughter. Then you will live according to your new identity.

You behave like you believe.

This truth will set you free from being a slave to sin and guilt. That's not who you are in Christ. You are a son or daughter of the King of the universe.

Now be free—indeed!

✳ ✳

Seek Truth

Today's Reading: John 8:39-47

HEARING GOD'S VOICE FOR TODAY:
"Why do you not understand what I say? It is because you cannot bear to hear my word. You are of your father the devil, and your will is to do your father's desires. He was a murderer from the beginning, and has nothing to do with the truth because there is no truth in him. When he lies, he speaks out of his own character, for he is a liar and the father of lies. But because I tell the truth, you do not believe me."

✳ ✳ ✳

All through Jesus' earthly ministry, many people did not understand his teachings. Their minds had been captured by his archenemy, the devil.

The same is true today. People refuse to listen to Jesus' teachings because their minds are under the authority of the enemy. They were born that way—the devil's evil wiles, schemes, and lies were hardwired in the human heart at the moment of conception.

The devil has been a murderer since the beginning of time. He was the one who incited Cain to kill his brother Abel. His job description is to kill, steal, and destroy anything the Father in heaven creates and wills.

The evil one is allergic to the truth. He is the father of lies. Lying began with him. He told Eve to doubt the Father's word as true. He contradicts God's character in every way. He can only operate out of his own lying nature. Every lie in creation is rooted in him. When he acts, he does so out of the core of his being.

What lies has the devil spoken to you? Has he nudged you toward feeling worthless? Has he hinted that you are hopeless? Has he suggested you can never change? Has he told you your circumstances are unalterable? Has he made you feel as though your life has no meaning?

Don't believe him. Believe Jesus. His character is rooted in eternal truth. He is the truth. It is who he is. It is what he speaks. It is his eternal nature. One of the major reasons he came to earth was to teach you this truth. He wants you set free from the tyranny of the father of lies. He wants you forever released from the one who desires to destroy you.

Know the devil's schemes. He studies you. He knows where you're weak. He tempts you so you will fall.

Believe today the truth that Jesus wants your health, happiness, and wholeness. He wants to give you abundant life. He is the strength of your heart and you belong to him forever. His mercies never cease. They are new every morning. He directs your steps and delights in every detail of your life.

And remember that all the pieces of the armor of God begin with the belt of truth. That must be the starting point. Without truth, the other pieces of the armor can't do much. Truth is the starting point and foundation for standing against the devil's schemes.

Reject all moral relativism. Embrace absolute truth. God authored it. And remember: Don't break his moral laws. When you disobey them, they break you.

The Lord's truth overcomes the father of lies. Find his truth. Live by it.

And you will be set free.

Jesus Is Your Provision Today

Today's Reading: John 8:48-59

HEARING GOD'S VOICE FOR TODAY:

"'Your father Abraham rejoiced that he would see my day. He saw it and was glad.' So the Jews said to him, 'You are not yet fifty years old, and have you seen Abraham?' Jesus said to them, 'Truly, truly, I say to you, before Abraham was, I am.' So they picked up stones to throw at him, but Jesus hid himself and went out of the temple."

✳ ✳ ✳

These words are among the most significant Jesus ever spoke. He told the Jews that Abraham rejoiced to see his day. The Father had promised Abraham that, through his son Isaac, all the nations would be blessed. Abraham had a joyful confidence that promise would come true.

Christ's death and resurrection unleashed the blessing of salvation upon all the nations, thus fulfilling the promise. During his life, Abraham looked forward to the day when this promise would be fulfilled. In heaven, he finally saw it fully realized.

The Jews still didn't understand. They objected loudly to this teaching, saying Jesus was not yet fifty years old and Abraham had lived a thousand-plus years earlier. How could Jesus have known him?

That's when Jesus made his clear claim to deity. There was no mistake about what he was saying. He claimed to have lived before Abraham. He existed in eternity before Abraham was ever conceived. He claimed transcendence over time—something only God could claim.

In Exodus 3:14, God gave Moses his name: "I AM WHO I AM." By saying, "Before Abraham existed, I AM," Jesus was claiming not only to be eternal, but the very God who appeared to Moses and told him his name.

The Jews had no doubt about what Jesus was saying. They "picked up stones" to kill him for blasphemy—the prescribed Old Testament punishment for false teaching. But he escaped, for his time for death had not yet come.

How will you respond to Jesus' claim to deity? The Jews understood his claim and wanted him eliminated. Is this your response? Not to make a decision about him is to make a decision. You are either on his side or against him. There is no neutrality when it comes to following him.

When you believe in Jesus and decide to follow him, you acknowledge he is the great I AM. He is not the great I WAS. Your past has been forgiven. He is not the great I WILL BE—though he perfectly oversees your future. He is the great I AM.

Whatever you are facing today is where he will be. He is your present help in all times of trouble. He is your sufficiency this moment. He is with you today—and all days. He asks that you have faith in him for today's worries alone. Tomorrow has enough worries of its own. He knows the price of fives sparrows—two copper coins. Yet he doesn't forget a single one of them when they fall to the ground. You are more valuable than sparrows. He knows the number of hairs on your head. He knows you intimately as well.

Believe it's true.

Because it is.

✳ ✳

There's Purpose in Pain

Today's Reading: John 9:1-7

HEARING GOD'S VOICE FOR TODAY:

*"As he passed by, he saw a man blind from birth. And his disciples
asked him, 'Rabbi, who sinned, this man or his parents, that
he was born blind?' Jesus answered, 'It was not that this man
sinned, or his parents, but that the works of God might be
displayed in him. We must work the works of him who sent
me while it is day; night is coming, when no one can work.'"*

✳ ✳ ✳

As Jesus and his disciples passed by a man born blind, they asked the
Lord a question based on a popular assumption of that day. They
wondered if the man was blind because of his sin or his parents' sin.
They believed wrongly that all human suffering is somehow connected
to a person's sin.

Their question was well-intentioned. They didn't want to connect
the Father with being the source of evil. They wanted to blame human
suffering on sin, not the Father in heaven.

But Jesus needed to correct their thinking. His life is an example
that shows that not all suffering is connected to sin. He was perfect and
sinless in every way, yet he experienced excruciating pain, rejection,
grief, and agony during his life on earth and on the cross.

Jesus told the disciples this man wasn't born blind because of his sin
or his parents' sin. Rather, the Father in heaven had permitted this so
his power and glory might be displayed through him.

What does this mean? Sometimes, God, in his mysterious prov-
idence, permits suffering that has no relation to sin. He does this so

people can experience and see the Father's extraordinary grace, mercy, and power delivering them from evil.

Yes, some suffering is caused by your sin. You may be paying the consequences for some bad choices you've made. Perhaps you broke the Father's moral law. There are consequences when we live life against his will.

Or perhaps someone else hurt you by no fault of your own. We live connected to one another. There is a necessary interdependence in this world. Consequently, someone else's bad choices can hurt us. Or maybe you just made a foolish mistake and are paying for it.

Whatever you may be going through today, trust Jesus. Know that he is a deliverer. He loves to show his power to people who are weak. He enjoys giving strength to weak hands and buckling knees. He heals the brokenhearted and bandages their wounds. He has compassion on your suffering. He comforts you in all your troubles. There's purpose in the pain.

If you believe this, you have the privilege of seeing him use evil for good. It gives you an opportunity to glorify him with greater gusto and zeal.

Jesus promised that he will share in your sufferings. His humanity allowed him to know what you are experiencing, feel what you are feeling. He mourns and cries with you. As you hurt, he hurts.

But he will never forsake you. His death and resurrection conquered all sin, suffering, and death.

Draw near to him today. He promises he will draw near to you.

Simple Obedience

Today's Reading: John 9:8-12

HEARING GOD'S VOICE FOR TODAY:
"He answered, 'The man called Jesus made mud and anointed my eyes and said to me, "Go to Siloam and wash." So I went and washed and received my sight.'"

* * *

After Jesus gave sight to the blind man, the man's neighbors didn't recognize him. Some said it was the blind man, now with sight. Others said it looked like him, but it was not him. But the blind man said repeatedly, "I am the man."

They asked, "Then how were your eyes opened?" He told his story. He shared how Jesus made mud and anointed his eyes. Then Jesus told him to go to the pool at Siloam and wash his eyes, and his sight would be restored. He did what he had been told to do, and his eyes were opened.

The blind man's testimony spoke loudly. Jesus came to change lives. All he asks is that you go share your changed life with others. They may want to argue doctrine, orthodoxy, or trivial Bible perspectives. But they cannot argue your testimony or your changed life. The blind man now saw. He shared this truth. That's all Jesus asks of you as well. Just share what happened to you. It's your best witness for him.

Please note as well that there is great power in simple obedience. The blind man obeyed what Jesus asked him to do, and the Lord used him mightily. It's a profound part of faithfully following him. You don't have to understand every fine point of theology to obey him. Just do what he tells you to do. Simply obey him—in all things great and small. And incredible results can follow when you do so.

Jesus' heart yearns for you to know his supernatural, unconditional, and healing love. He longs for you to know his life-changing eternal grace, mercy, and compassion. When you know these things inside you, there is no problem or obstacle you can't face in your life.

If you love the Lord, you will desire to obey all that he has commanded you to do.

There may be some days you don't feel like it. Obey him anyway. There may be some times your circumstances are daunting and you're tempted to take the easy way out. Obey him anyway. There may be times when peer pressure tempts you to follow the crowd and not him. Obey him anyway.

Simple obedience. It will tell others how he has changed your life. Don't be ashamed of what he has done for you. Do every small thing he asks you to do—even if it seems as silly as putting mud in your eyes and washing it off in a pool. Faith and obedience are undeniably connected.

And remember that the Lord withholds no good thing from those who do what is right. Joyful are those who obey his will and search for him with all their hearts. Desire that your actions consistently reflect God's will. There should be no shame when you compare your life with his commands.

If you want to increase your faith, obey Jesus. When you do, your faith will grow. Miracles will increase.

And he will be glorified.

Obedience Flows from His Love

Today's Reading: John 9:13-17

HEARING GOD'S VOICE FOR TODAY:
*"Some of the Pharisees said, 'This man is not from
God, for he does not keep the Sabbath.'"*

* * *

The blind man Jesus had healed was taken to the Pharisees. They were the leaders and watchdogs over Jewish propriety regarding the Law. They were exceedingly upset that Jesus had given sight to him on the Sabbath.

When the Lord used saliva to make the mud to put on the blind man's eyes, the Jewish leaders made an association with one of their 39 classes of work forbidden on the Sabbath. This was in accordance with the Mishnah—what the Jewish leaders used to interpret the Law. They continued to carefully quiz the man—looking for any reason to condemn Jesus.

Why do people try to reduce God's love and compassion to rules and regulations? The Father in heaven's relationship with the Israelites began in intimacy with their deliverance from Egyptian slavery. The Law, given at Mount Sinai, was given after the relationship with him was established. Grace came first. Then came the Law.

But instead of the Law being a means to an end, it became the end itself. Making sure no work was done on the Sabbath became more important than giving sight to a man born blind. The Jewish leaders failed to understand that the Sabbath was made for man—to help him worship God and rest—not man for the Sabbath. It was a gift from the Father.

How easy it is for this to happen to Jesus' followers! He desires to enter into a personal, living, and dynamic relationship with you. He wants you to know him intimately and experience his great grace. Obedience to his Law flows from this relationship.

But some people continue to reduce his grace to rules and regulations. They form a spiritual checklist—Bible study, prayer, fasting, service, church attendance—check, check, check, check, check. Then they think they've been faithful.

How sad! A living relationship is reduced to a list of do's and don'ts. Eventually your heart will harden. Your love will vanish like a vapor before the morning sun. A scowl will replace a smile. Your shoulders will become heavy and your heart weary. You will always wonder if you are ever doing enough to please the Lord.

Come to him today. Know how much he cares for you. Believe that his most important priority is a personal relationship with you. He is your friend. Know how much he loves you. In response, love him with all your heart, soul, mind, and might. Then love your neighbor as you love yourself.

Loving God and your neighbor is the encapsulation of all the Law. As you do these two things, you'll discover a lifetime's worth of work to do.

And your life will have meaning like never before.

✳ ✳

All Things Are Possible with God

Today's Reading: John 9:18-23

HEARING GOD'S VOICE FOR TODAY:
*"The Jews did not believe that he had been blind and
had received his sight, until they called the parents of
the man and asked them, 'Is this your son, who you
say was born blind? How then does he now see?'"*

✳ ✳ ✳

Why is it so difficult for people to believe in Jesus? Why do they try to find every possible excuse to deny he can accomplish the impossible? Why do they keep seeking human reasons to explain away his miraculous power?

That's what happened here after he healed the man born blind. The Jewish leaders wouldn't accept the miracle. They went to the parents of the man to find out if he really had been born blind. They couldn't accept that Jesus had given sight to a man born blind, a man who possessed a simple and obedient faith. That's because they had no faith.

What is faith?

Faith is the assurance of things hoped for, the conviction of things not seen. By faith, people believe that the Father in heaven created the world with a word. He made it from things not visible. Without faith, it is impossible to please God. Whoever wants to have a deep faith must not only believe that he exists, but that he rewards those who diligently seek him.

Faith never looks at the size of the mountain in one's path, but the size of the God who rules over all. And it's not the size of your faith that's important. If you have faith even the size of a mustard seed, you can say to a mountain, "Move from here to there," and it will move.

Faith believes that all things are possible with God. It believes that the God who miraculously created the world can still do the miraculous to achieve his divine purposes.

Faith believes that the Father in heaven can create a dry path through a large sea, make the sun stand still, feed thousands with five loaves and two fish, calm a storm with a word, heal the blind and the lame, and raise someone from the dead.

Do you have this kind of faith? Diligently seek the Father in heaven. Believe in him. Believe also in Jesus.

Believe that the Father wants to give you good gifts. If earthly fathers, who are inherently evil, love to give good gifts to their children, how much more does the heavenly Father love to give good gifts to his children who totally trust him?

Speak to the mountains that hinder you about the greatness of your God. Tell them to dissolve into the heart of the sea. Stop permitting the size of life's mountains to determine your life's destination. Dismiss destructive doubt. Trust in the Lord's miraculous power and realize that life's most beautiful vistas are found at the top of the highest mountains.

He will keep in perfect peace all those who trust in him, all those whose thoughts are fixed on him.[1]

Today, believe that Jesus is able to do more than you could ever think or imagine.

All things are possible with God.

Remain Connected to Jesus

Today's Reading: John 9:24-34

HEARING GOD'S VOICE FOR TODAY:
*"Never since the world began has it been heard that
anyone opened the eyes of a man born blind. If this
man were not from God, he could do nothing."*

✳ ✳ ✳

Jesus healed a man born blind. The man then defended Jesus against the Jewish officials. He didn't exaggerate in his assessment of the Lord. Since the world had been formed, no one had ever heard of anyone opening the eyes of a man born blind. He said correctly that this miracle could not have happened if Jesus was not sent from his Father in heaven.

Then the man made an extraordinarily insightful statement. If Jesus was not sent from God, he could do nothing. Unless his life was securely connected to the life of the Father in heaven, he had no authority. He could perform no miracles. He could not cast out demons. He could not preach the power of the kingdom of God.

Jesus, the Son, is in the Father. The Father is in him.

You cannot bear fruit in your own strength. Human strength cannot accomplish divine work. Apart from Jesus, no work possesses eternal value.

You need to abide in him. You must have a close, personal, living, dynamic, and vibrant relationship with him. You must remain connected to him throughout your day.

That's why prayer at all times is so important. It allows you to constantly communicate with Jesus and he with you. In prayer, you lean on him—totally dependent in all areas of your life. As you spend time in his Word, it will come to dwell richly in you. Worship will spontaneously happen whenever a thought about him crosses your mind. Obedience to his will becomes a joy as you serve the one you dearly love.

The very power that raised Jesus from the dead now lives in you. You have an eternal relationship with him. All your strength comes from being connected to him, the sovereign Lord of the universe. He makes you as sure-footed as a deer climbing to new heights. He gives power to the weak and makes them strong.

Have you ever wondered why he gives you so many blessings? There is a simple answer. He wants to bless you so that you can be a blessing to others.

Jesus wants to use you to give food to the hungry. He wants you to provide water to the thirsty. He wants you to be his presence to prisoners and the shut-ins. He would like for you to help those caught in human trafficking to be free. He desires you to be a funnel of hope to the hopeless. He wants you to be a vessel of love to the unloved.

Apart from him, these things can't be accomplished. But when you are connected to him, you can do anything.

Believe it's true.

God's strength becomes your strength.

Then act in his strength.

Let Jesus Find You

Today's Reading: John 9:35-41

HEARING GOD'S VOICE FOR TODAY:
"Jesus heard that they had cast him out, and having found him he said, 'Do you believe in the Son of Man?' He answered, 'And who is he, sir, that I may believe in him?' Jesus said to him, 'You have seen him, and it is he who is speaking to you.' He said, 'Lord, I believe,' and he worshiped him."

✳ ✳ ✳

The man born blind had been cast out of the synagogue. Jesus sought him, and found him. That's how he always works with people. Long before they ever seek him, he was seeking them. He is constantly knocking on the door of people's hearts.

You love Jesus because he first loved you. This is how his love works—not that you love him, but that he first loved you and gave his life as an atoning sacrifice for your sins. Long before you chose him, he had chosen you—before the world was ever formed.

Jesus found the blind man he had healed. The Jewish officials had rejected him. He'd been thrown out of the Temple. He needed Jesus' grace and mercy as all despised and rejected people do. The Lord knew how the man felt. He was treated that way too.

Jesus began a dialogue with him. It led to a true revelation of who he is.

Jesus asked the man if he believed Jesus was the Son of Man. The man knew this term was a reference to the long-awaited Savior of the Jews. He asked where this person was. Jesus told him it was the Son of Man who was speaking to him.

Humbly, the man said, "Lord, I believe." Note he called Jesus "Lord," a term of great respect. With this term, he recognized Jesus' identity. He knew Jesus to be God.

Then he worshiped Jesus. And the Lord received his worship. As the Son of Man, the Savior of the world, he could rightly receive this worship. Yes, only God is worthy of worship. But the Father and the Son are one. Jesus could receive this man's worship because he is God.

Do you believe Jesus Christ is God? In this encounter with the man born blind, you can see how he eventually came to recognize Jesus' deity. At first he thought Jesus was a mere man (verse 11). Then he thought Jesus was a prophet (verse 17). Finally, he realized Jesus was the Son of Man and worthy of worship (verse 38). Slowly, progressive revelation happened. He believed. And he worshiped.

Know who Jesus is. He is worthy of your worship. He created you and the world in which you live. Through him, all things came into being. All is under his sovereignty—including your life. He knows all. He sees all. He controls all.

He will even use your painful rejection for your good.

He is seeking you. He desires to have an intimate relationship with you. He wants you to trust him with everything in your life.

Please stop running and hiding from him.

Let him find you.

Jesus Is Your Shepherd

Today's Reading: John 10:1-7

HEARING GOD'S VOICE FOR TODAY:
*"He who does not enter the sheepfold by the door but climbs in by
another way, that man is a thief and a robber. But he who enters
by the door is the shepherd of the sheep. To him the gatekeeper opens.
The sheep hear his voice, and he calls his own sheep by name and
leads them out. When he has brought out all his own, he goes before
them, and the sheep will follow him…I am the door of the sheep."*

✳ ✳ ✳

In Jesus' day, a sheepfold was a common courtyard near or beside a
house. One of several family members would oversee all the sheep.
There was a specific door by which the sheep would enter the sheepfold. A gatekeeper would carefully guard the door. It could be a family
member or a hired hand.

Jesus is that door to the sheepfold. Those who enter through him
are God's children.

The gatekeepers are ministers and shepherds who are called by him
to oversee his sheep. Their job is to guard and feed his sheep.

Through the ages, thieves have tried to approach Jesus' sheep without going through him. Sometimes they pretend to be sent from him.
They try to fleece, not feed, his sheep. They try to use, not serve, his
sheep—for their own glory. His heart is broken when this occurs.

That is why you must learn to hear his voice. You must know his
Word and be able to discern true teachers from false ones. False teachers do not have your good as their highest aim. True teachers do. They

will continually point you to Jesus. They want him alone to receive all the glory. Self-aggrandizement and greed are not their desires.

Jesus is your shepherd. When you enter the sheepfold through him, you will want for nothing. He will lead you beside still waters and green grass. He will restore your soul.

He will lead you on the path of righteousness so that his name alone will be glorified. He doesn't share his glory with any human. You will desire that he alone receives all glory.

Should you walk through the valley of the shadow of death, you will never fear. Jesus promises to be with you. He will guide, comfort, and protect you. His living, personal presence in your life is the best antidote for fear of death. You will never walk alone.

He will prepare a banquet table for you in the presence of your enemies. He will soothe your frenzied life with his refreshing, soothing oil.

Your cup will overflow with his grace.

Surely his goodness and mercy will pursue you every day of your life. And you will dwell with him in the eternal dwelling place he has prepared for you.

Jesus will go before you. He will speak to you while leading you. Just let him be your Shepherd. Be guided by the good and faithful shepherds who love him—and faithfully teach his Word. And flee the false shepherds who are using you for greed and fame. They are not from Jesus.

Jesus' good shepherds want only your best—and his glory. Be sure to follow them.

✳ ✳

Jesus Died for You

Today's Reading: John 10:8-15

Hearing God's Voice for Today:

*"The thief comes only to steal and kill and destroy. I came that
they may have life and have it abundantly. I am the good
shepherd. The good shepherd lays down his life for his sheep."*

✳ ✳ ✳

The thief is God's eternal enemy. He has a very simple job description: To kill, steal, and destroy anything created by the Father in heaven. All this evil comes from him. He inaugurated the Fall in Genesis 3. Evil did not come from the Father.

Jesus' job description is exactly the opposite of the enemy's. He came into the world to give you abundant life. He doesn't call his followers to a miserable, depressed existence. He came for you to possess a rich, loving, encouraging, and joyful life. He wants his favor and blessing to flow through you to a hurting world.

All this comes when you enter into his sheepfold through him and have a personal, close, and intimate relationship with him.

Jesus is your good shepherd. This is the fourth time in John's Gospel he used the term "I AM." It's another claim to deity.

Note also that he describes himself as "good." He *is* good. It's an essential part of his nature. He wants his goodness to flow from his heart to yours. When life is difficult, always believe that he is working everything in your life for good—even the painful parts. Trust him that all is working together for your good because he is good. It's his character. It's who he is.

Finally, Jesus is your good shepherd. He loves you passionately.

How can you be certain of his love? It's because he is willing to lay down his life for his sheep—and for you. He literally gave his life on the cross for your sins to be forgiven so that you can have a personal relationship with him. Now you can live an abundant life rooted in his grace.

Don't assign to Jesus what the enemy has brought to you. The evil one wants to kill, steal, and destroy everything good in your life. He is not a good shepherd. Rather, he prowls around like a roaring lion, looking for someone to ravage. His power is great. He functions through hate. But resist him, and he will flee. Though he is a formidable foe, he is a defeated foe.

Remember that Jesus willingly gave up his life for you. Look at his cross. Survey his bloodied, bruised, and broken body. Remember his crown of thorns and his nail-scarred hands. Study his wounded side and pierced feet. This picture proves his love—it confirms he is the good shepherd.

You were once far away from God. You were his enemies, separated from him by your evil thoughts and actions. But now you are reconciled to God through the death of Jesus in his physical body. As a result, you are now brought into his own presence and declared holy, blameless, and without fault.

What good news! What an amazing expression of God's love to you. If you are a believer, his love now lives in you.

And when God's love pulsates through you, you will experience the abundant life he intended for you to have.

It can be yours today.

It's the reason he put on human flesh—so he could come for you and make you his own.

The Charge to God

Today's Reading: John 10:16-21

HEARING GOD'S VOICE FOR TODAY:

"I have other sheep that are not of this fold. I must bring them also, and they will listen to my voice. So there will be one flock, one shepherd. For this reason the Father loves me, because I lay down my life that I may take it up again. No one takes it from me, but I lay it down of my own accord. I have authority to lay it down, and I have authority to take it up again. This charge I have received from my Father."

* * *

As the Jewish leaders listened to Jesus, they could not grasp what he was saying. He told them there would be other sheep in his sheepfold who would not be Jewish.

He was referring to Gentiles. His message of grace and forgiveness of sins would be for all people around the world—including Gentiles. Even the prophet Isaiah had said so some 600 years earlier (Isaiah 56:8). But they had missed this charge. Now Jesus has given this command to his followers.

Jesus was looking forward to the day when there would be one worldwide flock under his guidance. This flock would be his church.

From the moment the Father asked the Son to leave heaven and come to earth, his vision was for both Jew and Gentile to be united as one in the church. The Holy Spirit would give birth to it. Different people from many different cultures and ethnicities would live in love and unity in it. What a glorious vision it was!

Jesus was sent by the Father to lay down his life for his sheep. It was his choice. He wasn't coerced. He intentionally submitted himself to the Father's will. The Father's heart danced with delight when he saw Jesus' voluntary submission to his desire.

Understand this truth: Jesus not only laid down his life, but he also took it up again. His divine nature was working in his resurrection. You can't keep a perfect God down. Death cannot defeat his love. Love will always conquer the power of sin and death.

His teaching also clearly answers the often-asked question, "Who killed Jesus?" Some suggest it was the Jewish leaders. Others say it was Pontius Pilate and the Roman authorities. Others say it was because of human sin that Jesus died. All these answers are partly true.

However, a key element of the answer is this: He chose to die. He willingly laid down his life for his sheep. That was his choice. By his authority, he chose to die and then be raised from the dead.

This was the Father's will for his life. Jesus gladly and willingly obeyed him. All this was done because of his great love for you.

Live for Jesus. Obey him as he obeyed the Father and laid down his life for you.

Go into the world and reach his sheep in different pastures. If you can't go physically, send money. It represents you. You spent long, laborious hours earning it. When it is sent, you are being sent.

And pray fervently that people will be drawn to Jesus. Pray that the Lord of the harvest will raise up laborers to go. The harvest is plentiful, but the laborers are few.

Just make sure you are going—in one way or another. As Jesus was sent from heaven, so he sends you into the world.

It's his great commission to all who follow him.

✳ ✳

You Can Hear Jesus' Voice

Today's Reading: John 10:22-30

Hearing God's Voice for Today:

*"My sheep hear my voice, and I know them, and they follow me. I
give them eternal life, and they will never perish, and no one
will snatch them out of my hand. My Father, who has given
them to me, is greater than all, and no one is able to snatch
them out of the Father's hand. I and the Father are one."*

✳ ✳ ✳

Take time to ponder these words from Jesus. Recall them in times
of distress and need. They include truths you can claim until your
dying breath.

His sheep hear his voice. He speaks to them throughout the day—
as a shepherd does his sheep. He knows each one by name. They know
his voice and respond to no one else.

He knows you by name. You should be able to discern his voice as
well.

How do you know when you are hearing his voice? It will always
be consistent with his Word. That's why it's imperative you know
Scripture.

When Jesus speaks to you, you will know what to do in every situation. And you will know how to follow him.

His greatest gift to his sheep is eternal life. This life is transitory.
Your few short years here can't begin to compare with eternity with
him. You receive the gift of eternal life by believing in him by grace
through faith.

If you are one of his sheep, no one will be able to snatch you out of his hand. You have eternal security. Because there was no work you did to earn your salvation, there is no work you can ever do to make him take it away. The Father gave you to the Son. You never have to worry about being separated from him. It will never happen.

The Father and the Son are one. That's another claim to his deity. Don't try to understand this truth. It's beyond human comprehension. Finite humanity cannot grasp this truth about the infinite. But it's true.

The Father and Jesus are eternally connected. When you come to Jesus, you become similarly connected. The super glue of his love eternally cements you together. Abide in his love.

Listen to Jesus' voice today. Be sensitive to it. If you need wisdom, ask him for it. He will give it to you generously—never rebuking you for asking for it. Make your plans, but trust that Jesus will determine your steps.

Jesus will guide you throughout your day and along the best pathway for your life. He will prompt you to go to people you should serve. He will warn you of all temptation. He will direct your paths and determine your steps. Should you go astray, seek him again, and he will place you back on the right path. He will guide you with his counsel. He will advise you and watch over you. He will lead you to your glorious destiny. He will watch over you until the day you die.

Jesus will whisper his unconditional love and guidance to you at all times. He has a grand plan and future for you life.

His sheep hear his voice.

Are you listening?

* *

Take the First Step

Today's Reading: John 10:31-39

HEARING GOD'S VOICE FOR TODAY:
*"If I am not doing the works of my Father, then do not
believe me; but I do them, even though you do not believe
me, believe the works, that you may know and understand
that the Father is in me and I am in the Father."*

* * *

Some of the people who saw Jesus doubted him. In a sense, they put him on trial. But when this happened, it wasn't him who was on trial. It was those who examined his life who were on trial. And the same is true about people today—including you.

In what way are you on trial? By the way you examine Jesus' works. By how you look at his miracles. One after another, they are paraded before you in Scripture. They all beg for an answer to this question: Who alone but God could perform such mighty works?

Examine them all. Look at the water being changed into wine. Look at those freed from the tyranny of demonic oppression—proving Jesus' power is greater than the devil's. Look at the thousands who were fed by him with only a paucity of food. The blind saw. The lame walked. The sick were healed. And the dead were raised.

Jesus performed these miracles to help those in need. They were signs for spiritual skeptics to believe in him—both then and now.

These signs show, beyond doubt, that the Father and the Son are one.

Have you carefully examined his miracles as revealed in his Word? When done, you will find that they speak loudly and clearly to his identity.

117

What else does this mean for you today? If the Father and the Son are one and you're a believer, then both live in you now. This is a promise for all who believe in Jesus. Think about this truth: The power that created the universe now lives in you!

More specifically, the fact they live in you means that you can face anything that comes your way. Their strength in you is greater than any problem you will confront. The Jesus who lives in you is greater than he, the devil, who lives in this world.[2]

What giant are you facing today? God is greater than the problem. Don't look at the size of your giants. Look at the size of your God who lives in you. And remember: God's fruit is most delicious where the giants are the biggest.

Now take the first step toward your problem. You can't be victorious if you stay put. As you do, strength will arise. You will gather supernatural momentum. You will discover you can do all things through the Lord as he gives you strength.

Trust him. As you keep moving forward, remember his miracles. They prove his power. He did them then. He still does them now.

Remember, Jesus can't steer a parked car. That's why you need to take the first step. No matter what the situation, God is your refuge and strength. He is always ready to help you in times of trouble. You should never fear when earthquakes come and the mountains crumble into the heart of the sea. His power is greater than your problem.

Experience his power flowing through you. And then watch your giants be slain—all for his glory!

* *

Let Jesus Guide You

Today's Reading: John 10:40-42

HEARING GOD'S VOICE FOR TODAY:
"He went away again across the Jordan to the place where John had been baptizing at first, and there he remained. And many came to him. And they said, 'John did no sign, but everything that John said about this man was true.' And many believed in him there."

* * *

As skeptics debated Jesus' identity, he brought several witnesses to his defense. He wanted to give them clear evidence supporting his claim to deity.

What were these witnesses? First, there were his miracles. Second, he had his Father's voice from heaven saying he was his Son—both at his baptism and at the Mount of Transfiguration. Finally, there was one more witness to his identity as God's Son: John the Baptist.

How was John a witness?

When Jesus arrived at a certain place across the Jordan, those who had followed him remembered this was where John had baptized many people—including Jesus. They remembered what John had said earlier about Jesus and concluded it was true.

What did John say about Jesus? He pointed to him and said, "Behold the Lamb of God who takes away the sins of the world." John told several of his disciples to leave him and follow Jesus. He said he was not worthy to tie the Lord's sandals. He said that he baptized with water but Jesus would baptize with fire—with the power of the Holy Spirit. He said that he needed to decrease in importance and Jesus must increase.

In all this, many skeptics came to believe in Jesus.

Do you still doubt who Jesus is? What more can be given to you as evidence that would help you to accept his true identity? If all this isn't enough to convince you, what else will?

When people honestly study his claims, they conclude he is who he said he is. They experience the new beginning he wants to give them.

More than anything else in the universe, Jesus wants you to know him. He wants you to have a personal, grace-filled relationship with him. He wants to give you a new life. He wants to indwell your heart. He wants to face every one of your life's problems with you—never forsaking you. He wants to guide you in everything you face.

Jesus especially wants to take you home to be with him forever. That's the major reason he came to earth: To seek and save that which was lost—yes, even you.

Let Jesus control your life. Seek his will in all you do, and he will show you which path you should take. He will work out his plans for your life. Yield to his guidance. You may make your plans, but he determines your steps. Follow him out of your darkness to light.

He is faithful.

He is who he said he is.

✳ ✳

Give God All the Glory

Today's Reading: John 11:1-4

HEARING GOD'S VOICE FOR TODAY:
"The sisters sent to him, saying, 'Lord, he whom you love is ill.' But when Jesus heard it he said, 'This illness does not lead to death. It is for the glory of God, so that the Son of God may be glorified through it.'"

✳ ✳ ✳

As people plotted to kill Jesus, he departed from Jerusalem. He went to Bethany, a city about two miles from Jerusalem on the eastern slopes of the Mount of Olives. Its name means "place of rest." It was such a place for him.

Jesus would go there regularly for rest from life's mounting pressures and be with very close friends: sisters Mary and Martha, and their brother, Lazarus. He loved them all—especially Lazarus.

As Jesus made his way to Bethany, Mary and Martha sent word to him that his close friend Lazarus was ill. Jesus already knew what would happen to Lazarus. He would die and then be resurrected. It would be a miracle that would show the glory of the Father working through his beloved Son.

Jesus' main purpose in performing miracles on earth was to show the greatness of his Father in heaven. He wanted to show the Father's true character—his love, kindness, mercy, and grace. He desired to give evidence of the Father's original intent for creation. God never designed for us to know disease, deformity, and death. They were evil intrusions into his once-perfect order. Jesus' miracles gave evidence of the Father's original design. They gave him glory regarding who he truly is.

When you rightly understand the Father's nature, your faith increases. You trust who he is as Jesus reveals him to you.

When Jesus does miracles today, he reveals the Father's glory.

Miracles aren't done for everyone, at any time, whenever they ask. Otherwise, people would look to Jesus as a genie in a bottle—wanting him to serve them at every whim or fancy. But the reason he came to earth was so we would learn that true life is found in being a servant. Jesus obeyed the will of his Father in heaven, and that's his desire for you as well.

When miracles occur, all glory should be given to God—where all glory is due. The Father does not share his glory with any human.

Do you believe that the Father alone deserves all the glory for what happens in your life? Do you have the phrase "To God alone be the glory" plastered in your mind? When you receive a compliment, or an award, or applause, do you give him the glory? When you consider creation, do you erupt in praise? When you ponder deep doctrinal truths, does your heart warm with gratefulness? Do you love to sing the doxology "Praise God from whom all blessings flow"?

When Jesus returns, he will receive glory from his people—praise from all who believe in him. If you believe in Jesus, this includes you.

That is the Lord's will for your life. He wants you to give him all the glory.

He alone is worthy to be praised.

Walk in Jesus' Light

Today's Reading: John 11:5-10

HEARING GOD'S VOICE FOR TODAY:

"Are there not twelve hours in the day? If anyone walks in the day, he does not stumble because he sees the light of this world. But if anyone walks in the night, he stumbles, because the light is not in him."

✳ ✳ ✳

Jesus warned his disciples that soon they'd have to return to Jerusalem. They objected. They knew the Jewish officials desired to kill Jesus because of his repeated claims to deity.

Jesus used their objections to teach a significant truth about following him.

He had already explained, "I am the light of the world" (John 8:12). When he invades your heart, his light enters you, and you become a light to the world. As his holy, eternal truth indwells your heart, his light shines through you.

Jesus will guide your paths with his light—no matter what the hour of the day may be. In the daytime, when there is light, it is easy to know where to walk. It's not difficult to walk when it's light. But when it's dark, you are more prone to stumble and fall.

When Jesus' light invades you, you can walk anywhere, at any hour of the day, and his light will guide you. That's what happens when you are in intimate fellowship with him. You are united together. He is in you, and you are in him. You hear his voice leading you. He shows you the next step. You obey what he tells you to do.

It's different for the person who is walking apart from Jesus. He is in the dark. He does not know the Lord's inward guidance. He doesn't seek his light, so truth doesn't indwell his heart. He has no desire to know Jesus. He does whatever he wants, whenever he wants. Because he walks in darkness, he will inevitably fall.

When Jesus walked to Jerusalem, he was walking from the light into darkness. He was following the Father's perfect plan. He was heading toward betrayal, arrest, torture, persecution, and eventual death on the cross. That was the Father's will, which Jesus desired to obey.

Does Jesus' light indwell you? Do you walk in his truth? Is your greatest desire to let him lead you to wherever he wants you to go? Is your most fervent desire to please him above all else?

If not, you are probably walking in darkness. You are most likely very far from him. Most assuredly, you will one day fall.

That is not the place where Jesus wants you to be. He is the light of the world. As his follower, he wants you to be a light on a hill, shining brightly for him. When others see your good works done for his glory, they will be moved to praise the Father in heaven.

Walk in Jesus' light at all times, in all places.

And as you follow him, his light that leads to life will lead you— every step of the way.

You Will Never Die

Today's Reading: John 11:11-15

HEARING GOD'S VOICE FOR TODAY:
*"Jesus told them plainly, 'Lazarus has died, and for
your sake I am glad that I was not there, so that
you may believe. But let us go to him.'"*

✳ ✳ ✳

Earlier, Jesus said that Lazarus had fallen asleep. The disciples took
Jesus literally. They thought Lazarus had entered into bodily sleep.
They failed to understand that "sleep" was a metaphor for death. Laza-
rus was dead.

Nor did the disciples understand what Jesus was about to do.

The Lord told them he was glad that he was not there when Lazarus died. Why did he say this? He wanted them to believe more deeply
after they saw what Jesus was about to do. When the disciples saw
how the Lord raised Lazarus from the dead, their faith would increase.
They would see that his delays don't mean his denials. Whenever they
remembered this event in the future, their faith would grow.

Then Jesus said it was time to go to Bethany, where they would witness the power and authority of his Father in heaven over everything
in the world—even death.

Believe in the Lord's power to do miracles. They are all around you.
Look at the birth of a child. Or ponder the beauty of a sunrise over the
horizon. Or consider the deep love you feel toward that special person in your life.

Theologians call these "common graces." They are available to all—
believers and skeptics alike. They are miracles surrounding you every

minute of every day. They are signs on your life's highway pointing you to God.

Jesus loves to do larger miracles as well. He revels in providing a way when there seems to be no way. He loves to open doors that seem closed. It gives him pleasure to move when all hope is gone. He still heals when doctors give up on you (like Lazarus!). He is able to give life to barren wombs. He enjoys paving ways where there seems to be no way.

Today, observe his miracles around you—both great and small. Remember his faithfulness to you. When you face obstacles, do so with the memory of his past faithfulness. You will be able to say, "If my Lord Jesus came through once for me, he can do it again." Trust that his delays don't mean his denials.

Especially remember this great miracle: Jesus raised Lazarus from the dead. As he did for Lazarus, he will do for all his followers. Your greatest miracle is yet to come. As Lazarus was raised from the dead, so will you be! When you die, he will take your lifeless body and give it a resurrection reality.

You have the absolute assurance that you will never die.

Because of what Jesus did on the cross, death has been defeated.

What a mighty promise and miracle!

Tell Jesus Your Feelings

Today's Reading: John 11:16-21

HEARING GOD'S VOICE FOR TODAY:
*"Martha said to Jesus, 'Lord, if you had been
here, my brother would not have died.'"*

✳ ✳ ✳

When Jesus finally arrived in Bethany, Lazarus had been in the tomb for four days.

In observance of Jewish tradition, mourners had come to the house. They grieved loudly with the family over the loss of Lazarus.

Martha heard Jesus was near. She met him outside the house and expressed her anger and disappointment in his delay. She said that if he had arrived earlier, her brother would not have died.

Jesus understood how Martha felt. And he understands when you are frustrated with him.

Everyone experiences dashed disappointments. When this happens, it's okay to express your feelings. They are in-built responders to life situations that surround you. God made your feelings. He placed them inside you.

There are two dangerous extremes to which you can go with your feelings. On one end of the continuum, you stuff them. You refuse to admit them. You pretend they are not present. This is very unhealthy to do. Eventually, it can cause depression.

Contrarily, you can dump them on everyone around you. This is unhealthy as well. People will flee from your presence. They won't want to deal with your negative emotions.

What is the answer? Go to Jesus with your feelings. Tell them to him. Cry out to him. Don't hold anything back. Tell him what's on your heart. David did this repeatedly in the Psalms. The Lord was not upset with him.

God comes to those who are crushed in spirit. He will not extinguish a flickering light, nor break a bruised reed. No matter how great our hurt, his comfort is greater.

Jesus is ready to handle your feelings. He wants you to come to him when you are weary from the load of heavy burdens. Go to him today if you are feeling anger and disappointment. Share your heart with him. Don't hold anything back.

Don't sin by letting frustration seethe within you. Don't let the sun go down on your anger. It gives a foothold to the devil. It's destructive to your soul. Tell Jesus all your hurts and despair. Be honest, as Martha was. He didn't become angry with her. And he won't be angry with you.

Let him carry your feelings. Cast them all upon him, for he cares for you. Don't hold any back. After you have suffered a little while, he will restore, support, and strengthen you. He will place you back on a firm foundation.

And you'll feel your burden melting away.

Your Eternal Destiny Is Secure

Today's Reading: John 11:22-27

HEARING GOD'S VOICE FOR TODAY:
*"Jesus said to her, 'I am the resurrection and the life. Whoever
believes in me, though he die, yet shall he live, and everyone who
lives and believes in me shall never die. Do you believe this?'"*

* * *

Martha had just told Jesus that she believed Lazarus would one
day be raised from the dead in the final resurrection. Jesus
responded that Lazarus would indeed rise again, for he was the resurrection and the life.

Yes, one day the Lord will launch the final resurrection. And that
brings us to this important truth: Resurrection life occurs only through
a relationship with Jesus. Whoever believes in him, though he die, he
will live. It's an extraordinary promise.

Believing in Jesus is not mere intellectual assent. It's much more.
When you believe in him, your life is yielded to him and united with
his. You are eternally connected. And as he lives his life through you,
you can then do all things through him who gives you strength. Jesus
is your life.

When you die, your mortal, fading, earthly body will be taken off—
like you take off your clothes at the end of the day. Your soul will then
be enwrapped in a new, perfect, glorified resurrection body that will
never die.

Don't miss this key "I am" statement from Jesus. He is the resurrection and the life. Whoever believes in him will never die. This
was another claim to deity. Moses never said this. Mohammed never

uttered such words. Nor did the Buddha or Confucius. It's a unique claim. Only Jesus made it. Only he could do that.

That's because Jesus was God in human flesh. Those who believe in him will never die.

Jesus asked Martha if she believed this. She said that she believed he was the Christ and the Son of God. She said she believed he was the one "who is coming into the world," a messianic expression from Psalm 118:26. She believed he was the fulfillment of all the Old Testament Scripture.

Do you believe these things about Jesus? He is your present help in time of trouble. He is your strong tower to whom you can run in times of distress. He is your protective shield who daily defends you against enemy assaults.

If you believe in Jesus, you know that this earthly tent in which you live will be taken down when you die. You will have a house in heaven, an eternal body made for you, made by God himself.

And Jesus is your resurrection hope. If you have received him, he has given you the right to become one of his children.[3] If you believe in him, you have eternal life. He is your assurance of life after death. He is your conviction that you will be with him in paradise.

To be absent from the body is to be with the Lord. Though you die, you live.

Settle the question of your eternal destination now, and you can live this life to the full.

Go to Jesus with All Your Hurts

Today's Reading: John 11:28-31

HEARING GOD'S VOICE FOR TODAY:
*"When she had said this, she went and called her sister Mary,
saying in private, 'The Teacher is here and is calling for you.'
And when she heard it, she rose quickly and went to him."*

✳ ✳ ✳

Jesus had just told Martha that he was the resurrection and the life. And her brother, Lazarus, would soon be raised from the dead.

Jesus wanted Martha's sister, Mary, to witness the miracle as well. He also wanted some time with her to encourage her grieving heart and reassure her of resurrection realities.

How Jesus loved Mary! She loved him as well. Her heart was exceedingly pure. Her faith was great. Jesus knew that as they spent time together, he could give her hope amidst her despair and soothe her hurting heart.

Jesus wants to do the same for you today. If your soul feels shattered, and your heart is hurting, and your insides crave healing, he wants you to know that his heart aches with yours. He feels what you are feeling. He desires to give you hope.

Therefore, go to him. Spend time in a quiet, private place with him. Perhaps it's a place where you've met before. Or perhaps it's where you meet regularly. He will be there to meet with you. He yearns to spend time alone with you today.

There is no burden you are carrying that he doesn't want to carry for you. There's no hurt in your heart he doesn't desire to heal. There is no pain you are experiencing with which he doesn't empathize. There is no disappointment in your life he doesn't want to help you overcome.

Jesus is a man of sorrows and acquainted with grief. There is no hurt or temptation common to you that he has not gone through. He overcame them all, and he can help you do the same. Nothing is impossible for him.

Go to Jesus today. Tell him what's happening in your heart, and make all your requests known to him. He loves your truthful, honest feelings expressed openly to him. He loves to lift the loads you are carrying. He is lifting you up now, carrying you. Even righteous people face troubles, and the Lord is faithful to rescue you when you come to him.

Jesus loves to bandage your wounds. He wants to give help to the fallen and discouraged. He desires to give you a double blessing for each one of your troubles.

Don't hesitate any longer. He is waiting for you. He desires some special time alone with you to hear your heart.

He really does care.

Grieve with Hope

Today's Reading: John 11:32-37

HEARING GOD'S VOICE FOR TODAY:
"He said, 'Where have you laid him?' They said to him, 'Lord, come and see.' Jesus wept. So the Jews said, 'See how he loved him!'"

* * *

When Jesus saw Mary and all the others weeping, he asked the question, "Where have you laid him?" He was then led to Lazarus's tomb.

And he wept. Many have noted that John 11:35 is the shortest verse in the Bible. It is. But that's not the reason it's especially noteworthy.

The fact that Jesus wept is important because it shows his followers how to handle grief.

He wept because of what death had done to his Father's once-perfect creation. He wept because of what death had done to his dear friend Lazarus. Death and destruction were never a part of the Father's original intent. They are evil intrusions into what was once perfect.

Please note Jesus' example of how to handle grief—especially when you lose a loved one. The apostle Paul wrote in 1 Thessalonians 4:13 that Christians should always grieve with hope. Grief is good. It's the Father's way of reminding you that there is much more after this life. Grief reminds you that eternity is your home and it is there that you will see your loved ones again. Only in heaven will all grief cease.

God wants you to grieve over your loss. It's human and natural. Someone once spelled grief L-O-S-S. As you go through life, you will begin to lose things and people you love. You will eventually leave everything in this world. And the more heartfelt the loss, the greater the grief is.

That's why tears are the Father's gift to you. They are his natural way to salve your soul. They cleanse the wounds in your heart. You need to grieve over your loss.

But don't stop there. Yes, grieve. But grieve with hope. One day, in eternity, you will be reunited with your loved one who trusted in Jesus. There is a better place awaiting you.

Jesus' followers grieve with hope. Those who don't believe in him can't grieve this way. Yes, you grieve—as all humans do with loss. But you grieve with an eternal hope. If your loved ones believed in him, you will see them again. Heaven is your home.

Jesus wept with grief when he experienced loss. He knew that tears are a gift from the Father to help salve raw emotions.

So should you. It's a gift to help your hurting heart.

But always remember to grieve with hope. It is hope that gives you the courage to face anything. And it is hope that reminds you that your grief is momentary in comparison to what awaits you in heaven.

For those who follow Jesus, death is merely an entrance into eternal life. It's not the end, but the beginning. Death has lost its sting.

It has no victory over those who believe in Jesus.

Jesus has won!

✳ ✳

Creating Something from Nothing

Today's Reading: John 11:38-44

HEARING GOD'S VOICE FOR TODAY:

*"Jesus said to her, 'Did I not tell you that if you believed you would
see the glory of God?' So they took away the stone. And Jesus lifted
up his eyes and said, 'Father, I thank you that you have heard
me. I knew that you always hear me, but I said this on account
of the people standing around, that they may believe that you
sent me.' When he had said these things, he cried out with a loud
voice, 'Lazarus, come out.' The man who had died came out."*

✳ ✳ ✳

Martha objected when Jesus gave the command to move the large
stone in front of the tomb. Lazarus had been dead for four days.
She was afraid the foul odor from his decomposed body would be overwhelming. Jesus reminded her that if she simply believed, she would
see the glory of God.

Note how the Lord prayed before he raised Lazarus. And let his
example aid your prayer life and increase its power.

First, Jesus lifted his eyes to heaven. That doesn't mean it's wrong
to bow your head and close your eyes. But when you lift your eyes to
heaven as you pray, you are reminded of the Father sitting on his sovereign throne. He alone has the ability to answer your request.

Second, Jesus thanked the Father. There's enormous power in
thanksgiving. Begin your prayers with thanksgiving. It shows your
humility and dependence upon God. You are also reminded of the
times God has come through for you in the past.

Third, the Father heard Jesus' pleas for Lazarus's resurrection. Believe that the Father hears your prayers too. He hears your pleas as well.

Jesus cried aloud, "Lazarus, come out." The imagery suggested here is that of a horse snorting and neighing on its hind legs as it approaches battle. Jesus was entering a battle against the powers and forces of darkness as he called for Lazarus to rise.

He didn't need to speak many words. In ages past, the omnipotent Father spoke, and creation sprang forth from nothing. Here, Jesus spoke three words, and Lazarus's dead body returned to life.

At the time of your salvation, Jesus did this same miracle for you. He spoke to your dead, lifeless heart and called out your name to give you new life. You were dead in your sins and trespasses, and he made you alive. Originally you were born of the flesh, and now you are born again of the Spirit.

There was no good work you could have performed to receive this new life. Dead hearts can't do anything to earn God's grace. It's a gift to you—received only through faith. That way, you can never boast, and the Father alone receives all the glory.

If Jesus spoke to your dead heart and made it alive, he can meet your needs today. Though your strength may fail, God will sustain you. He is able to give you whatever you may need. He possesses all power. He loves to make all things new.

He loves to create something from nothing.

Just give all your burdens to him. Stand on his promises. Trust his words.

✳ ✳

Love the Church

Today's Reading: John 11:45-53

HEARING GOD'S VOICE FOR TODAY:
"Caiaphas, who was high priest that year, said to them, 'You know nothing at all. Nor do you understand that it is better for you that one man should die for the people, not that the whole nation should perish.'...He prophesied that Jesus would die for the nation, and not for the nation only, but also to gather into one the children of God who are scattered abroad."

✳ ✳ ✳

Lazarus had been raised from the dead. The Jewish leaders weren't happy about this and gathered to contemplate what to do with Jesus. As the people's zealotry for Jesus surged, the leaders were fearful that Rome would take away their power, control, and authority.

Caiaphas was the high priest. He had been a high priest for a long time and was proud and arrogant.

Eerily, Caiaphas prophesied about Jesus' work on the cross. He said it was better for one man to die for the sake of an entire nation.

John saw a double entendre in Caiaphas's unwitting prophecy. It not only looks forward to Jesus' death for the salvation of Israel, but to others scattered around the world. He anticipated a day when both Jew and Gentile would be gathered together in a place called the church.

The church is a unique family—one never divided by age, gender, color, economics, or social barriers. Jesus tore down the restraining walls that have kept people apart. There is equality, love, peace, and unity among them in his church. He loves it when his church has many different colors and backgrounds in it.

Are you a part of a local church family? You should be. You need to connect yourself to other followers of Jesus who will love, encourage, care for, and pray with you. You need to be able to confess your sins and share your burdens with others. You should make yourself available to help other members of God's family in these ways as well.

If you remove a piece of charcoal from a fire, it will eventually go out. But when it remains in the fire with other pieces of charcoal, it will glow for a long time.

Likewise, you need others to help your faith remain strong. And you need to help others grow in their faith.

Jesus loves his church. You can't say you love him and not love that for which he gave his life. That's like telling a husband who is madly in love with his wife, "I really like you, but I don't like your wife." If you truly liked him, you would like his wife too because of his great love for her.

If you truly love Jesus, you must love that which he loves most in the world: his Bride. The church is his new creation. From heaven he came and sought her to be his holy Bride. And with his blood he purchased her. And for her life he died.[4]

Jesus is the head of the church and lives in her to serve this dying world. His Bride is a church triumphant, one that will live with him forever.

Jesus loves his church, his Bride.

Make sure you're involved in one of his local families.

Seek Jesus First

Today's Reading: John 11:54-57

HEARING GOD'S VOICE FOR TODAY:
*"Now the Passover of the Jews was at hand, and many went
up from the country to Jerusalem before the Passover to
purify themselves. They were looking for Jesus and saying
to one another as they stood in the temple, 'What do you
think? That he will not come to the feast at all?'"*

✳ ✳ ✳

Hostilities were rising against Jesus. He knew the chief priests and
Pharisees wanted to arrest him. But he knew the time of his arrest
needed to wait until the end of the Passover. So he went to Ephraim to
wait for the right time.

Many people were looking for Jesus in Jerusalem. Recognizing the
increasing angst against him, they wondered if he would come to Jerusalem at all. But at least they were seeking him.

Which brings us to this very important truth: If you seek, you will
find. If you ask, there will be an answer. If you knock, the door will be
opened.

Seeking the Lord is not a one-time search. It's persistent. It doesn't
give up easily. He rewards perseverance in prayer.

Consider this analogy: Earthly fathers' hearts are tainted with selfishness. Like all people, they've inherited a disease called sin. Yet no
matter how selfish they are, earthly fathers still love to give good gifts
to their kids.

If that's true, (and it most assuredly is), then we can argue from the
lesser to the greater: How much more does the heavenly Father want

to give good gifts to you, his very own child? He is a good Father who is generous beyond words. He rewards those who diligently seek him.

But you must first seek him with all your heart, soul, mind, and might. And remember: His best gift is his presence, not presents.

Are you seeking him today? The Father will not coerce you to seek him. That's your choice. He desires it. But he won't force it to happen.

Sadly, too many people seek mostly after the things of this world—possessions, power, and pleasures. These things don't last. They are all left here when you die. You enter and leave the world naked. You will never see a U-Haul trailer attached to a hearse.

If you are a believer, when you die, you will take the Father's presence with you into eternity. That's what lasts forever. You won't take one present with you. Today, invest in your relationship with him. That's the highest priority

Seek first the Father and his kingdom. That's what lasts forever. When you do, he will supply your every earthly need according to his heavenly riches.

And everything else in this world will grow increasingly dim.

Serve the Poor

Today's Reading: John 12:1-8

HEARING GOD'S VOICE FOR TODAY:
"Jesus said, 'Leave her alone, so that she may keep it for
the day of my burial. For the poor you always have
with you, but you do not always have me.'"

✳ ✳ ✳

Mary had just expressed complete devotion to Jesus by anointing his head and feet with expensive perfume. It was valued at around a year's salary.

Judas objected loudly. He said the perfume should have been sold so this large amount of money could be given to the poor. But John noted in his Gospel that Judas was not concerned for the poor. Rather, Judas didn't want money wasted that he could possibly pilfer from their treasury.

Jesus told Judas to leave Mary alone. He had no right to condemn her for her benevolent act. Indeed, when anyone would read about Mary's act in the future, it would serve to remind him of what true devotion to the Lord looks like.

Jesus then told Judas that the poor would always be in their midst. He was alluding to Deuteronomy 15:11—the reality that poverty will exist on earth until he returns again.

The causes of poverty are many. Some people are poor because of their irresponsible, indolent choices. Others are the working poor, who try very hard to make ends meet each day. They are desperately trying to keep their head above water. Others are true victims of economic disasters, war, genocide, or diseases. Still others are trapped in a sinister system and cycle of poverty.

No matter what the causes, Jesus calls us to care for those who are broken, powerless, and voiceless. Unless they are able-bodied and refuse to work, we are called to help them. And remember this teaching from Jesus himself: When you look into their faces, remember you are looking into his face. When you serve them, you are serving him.

Jesus wants you to be his hands and feet to the poor around the world. One of the names of his church is "the body of Christ." On earth, you are Christ's representative to broken people. Your feet are his feet taking you to them. Your hands are his hands touching their needs. Your voice is his voice giving them hope.

One day, Jesus will return and eradicate all poverty. None of his children should be hungry, thirsty, sick, or destitute. In his soon-arriving kingdom, there will be perfect righteousness and justice. Every need will be met. Every body will be healed. Every heart will be whole. Every person will be fed. Those who thirst will be satisfied.

There will be no poverty at all.

Until that day, pray and work hard to advance Christ's kingdom on earth. When he returns, let him find you working for this end— especially among the poor.

If you help the poor, you are lending to the Lord—and he will repay you! When you feed the poor and help those in trouble, your light will shine forth in the darkness.

And when you look into the faces of the poor, you will see the face of Jesus.

To serve the poor is God's will for you today—until Jesus comes again and the poor will no longer be among you.

✳ ✳

You Are What You Think

Today's Reading: John 12:9-11

HEARING GOD'S VOICE FOR TODAY:
*"When the large crowd of the Jews learned that Jesus was there,
they came, not only on account of him but also to see Lazarus,
whom he had raised from the dead. So the chief priests made
plans to put Lazarus to death as well, because on account of
him many of the Jews were going away believing in Jesus."*

✳ ✳ ✳

Jesus returned to Bethany to visit with Mary, Martha, and Lazarus. A large crowd assembled at their house. They wanted a glimpse of both Lazarus and Jesus. Lazarus had become a local celebrity, the person whom Jesus had raised from the dead.

People love to worship human celebrities. They are prone to exalt creatures over the Creator.

Contrarily, the religious leaders were repulsed by Lazarus's resurrection. Their power base was being threatened because the masses were choosing to follow Jesus. Therefore, they decided to get rid of the evidence of the miracle and made plans to kill Lazarus.

Some people will do whatever is necessary to deny obvious truth. Even though a living, breathing Lazarus was before them, offering undeniable proof of Jesus' identity as the Son of God, they refused to believe in him. They would rather destroy Lazarus's life than change their lives and follow Jesus.

Sin is never rational. Though creation cries out that the Father exists, people still refuse to believe. Though Jesus' abundant miracles pointed clearly to his identity as the Son of God, people refused to believe.

Never underestimate the power of sin to delude your ability to think correctly. You can convince yourself of anything if you want something badly enough. Be very careful. This is a dangerous state in which to be.

The power of sin yearns for control and self-aggrandizement. It always desires to worship the creature rather than the Creator. This leads to irrational thinking that motivates godless behavior.

When Jesus changes a life, the first thing he changes is the mind. That's what he did with you. He altered the way you think. You have been transformed by the renewal of your mind. As you think in your heart, so you are. Your behavior, feelings, and actions follow your thought life. Belief influences behavior.

When you learn to think as he thinks, you will live as he lived.

Whatever is honorable, just, pure, lovely, commendable, excellent, and worthy of praise—think on these things. Flood your mind with positive, grace-filled thoughts. Set it on things that are above in heaven.

When you do, you'll find your behavior will change.

That's because you are what you think.

One Day You Will Understand

Today's Reading: John 12:12-19

HEARING GOD'S VOICE FOR TODAY:
*"His disciples did not understand these things at first, but when
Jesus was glorified, then they remembered that these things
had been written about him and had been done to him."*

* * *

As Jesus entered Jerusalem, crowds shouted, "Hosanna! Blessed is
he who comes in the name of the Lord." He was riding on a don-
key—the fulfillment of a prophecy in Zechariah 9:9. Palm branches
were waved at him and placed in his path—a reception traditionally
reserved for Roman conquerors. The people thought Jesus was a military presence who would soon vanquish all oppression.

The disciples did not understand what all this meant until after Jesus'
death and resurrection. Not until they had put together all the pieces
of the puzzle did they finally realize the significance of this moment.
Looking back, they came to realize that Christ's kingdom was not military in nature, but spiritual. They understood that his message was that
of a shepherd-king conquering human hearts. It would be a conquest
of internal choice, not external force.

The crowd had gathered because Jesus had raised Lazarus from the
dead. Wanting a glimpse of the one who had done this miracle, they
lined the road into Jerusalem. Like the disciples, many of them would
not understand Jesus' mission and how he would accomplish it until
after his death and resurrection.

Frequently, spiritual truth is seen in hindsight. Sometimes you
won't understand what God is doing in your life. You'll be confused

and tempted to become bitter. The nasty head of unbelief will rear itself as you cry out angrily to God, "Why? What are you doing?"

It is in such times that you need to continue to trust him. Believe he is at work—especially when you can't see it. Many people of great faith have learned that often God is on a multiyear plan.

What does that mean? Wait a few years. Commit to trusting him as you wait. Then look back at your life and see what he was doing. You'll see pieces of his plan falling into place. You'll begin to comprehend how he was turning your mess into a message. You'll see his tests were meant for a stronger testimony. You'll understand that a dark valley's purpose was to give you a grander vision.

The Lord knows that today's difficulties seem hard. He understands your path is not easy. He recognizes that living in the fog of the unknown can be challenging—sometimes seemingly impossible.

Continue to trust him. Commit yourself to waiting. He hears your cries. He is a faithful God. He will not delay forever. Endure patiently. God has not forgotten you. He rescues the godly. He is your fortress in times of trouble. Trust him in your pain.

Today, you look into a mirror dimly. Later, you will see more clearly.

And in heaven, you will see him face to face and understand everything with perfect clarity.

✳ ✳

The Purpose of Brokenness

Today's Reading: John 12:20-26

HEARING GOD'S VOICE FOR TODAY:
*"Philip went and told Andrew; Andrew and Philip went
and told Jesus. And Jesus answered them, 'The hour has
come for the Son of Man to be glorified. Truly, truly, I say
to you, unless a grain of wheat falls in to the earth and
dies, it remains alone; but if it dies, it bears much fruit.'"*

✳ ✳ ✳

Some Greeks wanted to meet Jesus. He wanted to meet them as well. His gospel is for everyone in the world—Jew and Gentile alike.

Philip brought the Greeks to Andrew. Andrew took them to Jesus. Andrew had a heart for bringing people to the Lord—for example, he had brought his brother, Peter. Now he was bringing Greeks. Oh, that we would all have Andrew's heart to introduce people to Jesus!

The Lord taught the Greeks something of extraordinary importance. He told them the hour had come for the Son of Man to be glorified. He knew that within a few days he'd be lifted up on the cross. His hour of humiliation and glory was near.

The term *glorified* means "weighted." It speaks of something being heavier or greater than something else—like iron being heavier than water. The glorified Jesus is greater than anything else in the universe. His cross and resurrection prove it.

When Jesus said a grain of wheat cannot bear much fruit until it falls into the ground and dies, he was speaking of his death on the cross. Only through his death could he grant new resurrection life for millions around the world.

He was speaking of your life as well. He was talking about the blessedness of brokenness. Only the poor in spirit understand his kingdom. Only those who weep will be comforted by the Holy Spirit, who indwells the hearts of all those who believe in him.

The only people who receive his resurrection hope are those who are broken. His resurrection life is only for those who have died to self and been crucified with him.

Have you died to self and been crucified with him? Have you experienced the blessedness of brokenness? Have life's distorted and bankrupt promises finally driven you to him?

If so, you should be glad. The kingdom of heaven can now enter your heart. The Holy Spirit who indwells you can comfort you. You now know that God loves the humble and stands against the proud. Humility precedes honor. The humble will see God work in powerful ways and be glad. They will inherit the earth.

The pain that you went through was the very instrument the Father in heaven used to draw you to him. It was necessary to break you of self-love.

Now Jesus can use you. Now he can bear much fruit through you.

It begins with being broken.

Rejoice in your pain, sorrow, and brokenness.

There's purpose in it.

Jesus Draws You to Himself

Today's Reading: John 12:27-36

HEARING GOD'S VOICE FOR TODAY:
*"Now is the judgment of this world; now will the ruler
of this world be cast out. And I, when I am lifted up
from the earth, will draw all people to myself."*

* * *

Jesus would soon go to the cross to die for the sins of the world. His Father's judgment on this world would soon come. All sins would be condemned forever.

But the Father had a plan. Instead of his wrath falling upon you, it fell upon his Son. Jesus became the penal substitute for your sins. Judgment fell upon him instead of you. He took the punishment he didn't deserve so he could give you the forgiveness you didn't deserve.

All this was done because of the Father's great love for you.

At the same time, when Jesus died, the ruler of this world, Satan, was cast out. He was forever defeated. The foul enemy of the Father and your soul was overcome. When you believe in Jesus, the devil has no more authority over you.

When Jesus was lifted up on the cross, he drew all people to himself. This doesn't mean everyone in the entire human race. Obviously, many people choose to reject his claims. They want only refuse to follow him.

This term "all people" means "all kinds of people"—that is, all kinds of people from all around the globe. Christ's kingdom will have Jews and Gentiles, rich and poor, young and old, male and female, and all skin colors.

This broad range of people and ethnicities will comprise his church.

They will love, encourage, serve, and pray for one another. Together, they will serve this hurting world until he comes again.

Jesus is the one who draws you. As you survey his wondrous cross, don't you sense his love drawing you? It's his amazing grace wooing you to come and follow him.

When you chose to follow Jesus, realize he was already drawing you. With every situation and circumstance, in every relationship, in every moment of your life, he has been drawing you. He does this so he can crown you with his tender mercies.

Jesus knew you by name when you were in your mother's womb. He knew your name even before the foundations of this world were ever laid. Though human parents may have dementia and forget your name, he never will. It's written indelibly in his mind.

He wanted you in his kingdom. His cross proves it. What more could he give?

Respond today to his great love. No eye has seen, no ear has heard, and no mind has imagined what God has prepared for those who love him.[5]

It's something that demands your soul and your life—indeed, your all!

✳ ✳

Fear God, Not People

Today's Reading: John 12:37-43

HEARING GOD'S VOICE FOR TODAY:
*"Many even of the authorities believed in him, but for fear of
the Pharisees they did not confess it, so that they would not be
put out of the synagogue; for they loved the glory that comes
from man more than the glory that comes from God."*

✳ ✳ ✳

Sometimes people miss the fact even many authorities came to
believe in Jesus. This included influential members of the Sanhedrin, like Nicodemus and Joseph of Arimathea.

Yet a major problem persisted. Though these authorities decided to
put their faith in Jesus, their fear of the Pharisees remained strong. They
were afraid to follow the Lord publicly for fear of being ostracized from
their synagogues. They knew they would face rejection. Not to be able
to have community with other Jews was a great fear.

The human heart is complex. People want to follow Jesus, but they
fear public rejection. They want to follow him, but they also want the
praises of people.

It's impossible to have both. Some people in your sphere of influence will not like you if you choose to follow Jesus. They will label you
a narrow-minded, bigoted obscurantist. They will call you intolerant.
They will hate you because you love Jesus. If you follow him, you must
be willing to give up the praises of people.

If you do make your faith in Jesus public, your reward in heaven
will be great. If you honor him before people, he will do the same with
you before the Father.

Your public recognition of Jesus here on earth will bring you rejection from some. But from an eternal perspective, it will be worthwhile. When you hear his public commendation of your witness before the Father, all the angels and saints in heaven will break out in uproarious applause.

That one moment will soothe all your hurts from people's rejection.

Don't be ashamed of the gospel. It is the power of the Father in heaven to change hearts—first to the Jews, then to the Gentiles. There is no such thing as a secret-service Christian. You should never want to remain quiet about all you've seen the Lord do and all he has done for you.

You are called to be his witness. You begin locally, then reach out globally.

Ask yourself this question often: If you were put on trial for being Jesus' witness, would the evidence be enough to convict you?

Don't fear what others can do to you. Yes, they are able to kill your body. But that's all. If you fear anything, fear God, who has the power and authority to cast both body and soul in hell. He will protect you from those who desire to do you harm.

His opinion is the only one that should concern you.

✳ ✳

You Are Forever Forgiven

Today's Reading: John 12:44-50

HEARING GOD'S VOICE FOR TODAY:

*"If anyone hears my words and does not keep them, I do not judge
him; for I did not come to judge the world but to save the world.
The one who rejects me and does not receive my words has a judge;
the word that I have spoken will judge him on the last day."*

✳ ✳ ✳

It is important that you learn to distinguish the reasons for Jesus' first
and second comings.

The first was his incarnation. He willingly and joyfully obeyed the
Father, who sent him into the world to die for the forgiveness of your
sins.

That was Jesus' sole reason for coming the first time. He did not
come to judge or condemn the world. He came to seek and save the
lost—to forgive people of their sins and give them eternal life.

But he will come a second time. When he returns, he will condemn
and judge this fallen world. He will eliminate all wickedness and bring
perfect justice. He will right all wrongs. No one will get away with sin.

Jesus will judge everyone. The one who has rejected him will not
enter into heaven. In fact, the words Jesus spoke will judge him. He
will know what Jesus said, and will be held responsible for his response.

If you have accepted Jesus as Lord and Savior, your judgment has
already taken place. The moment you accepted his forgiveness, you
were pronounced, "Not guilty."

There is no condemnation for those who are in Christ. If you ever
hear a voice accusing you of wrong, it's not the Lord's voice.

How can you know this is true? Because when you accepted Jesus, he accepted your condemnation. On the cross, he took the rejection you deserved and gave you the Father's acceptance that you didn't deserve.

It's all a free gift given to you through his grace and mercy. It can't be earned. There is nothing you can do to deserve it.

You are given eternal life. When you live to please the Spirit, you will harvest everlasting life from him. When you die and leave this earth, you have an eternal body made for you by the Father himself and not by human hands.

Live today in that eternal reality. Bask in the gracious glow of God's grace. The Lord is slow to anger and filled with unfailing love, forgiving every kind of sin and rebellion. Your sins are forever blotted out, and he will remember them no more.

Yes, you are forgiven. Your judgment has already happened. It's a gift from the Lord because of his great love for you.

You are loved in the Beloved—and the Beloved is Jesus.

Called to Serve

Today's Reading: John 13:1-5

HEARING GOD'S VOICE FOR TODAY:
*"He laid aside his outer garments, and taking a towel, tied
it around his waist. Then he poured water into a basin
and began to wash his disciples' feet and to wipe them
with the towel that was wrapped around him."*

✳ ✳ ✳

The Jews had rejected Jesus. It was the night before he went to the cross. He was nearing the Father's appointed time to die.

As you read about his preparation for the cross, keep in mind these three points:

First, because the Jews had rejected Jesus, he was now devoting his full attention to those who had faithfully followed him to the end. Through them, he was going to start a movement that would change the world. They were now his focus.

Second, the devil had put into Judas's heart the desire to betray Jesus. Satan was the tempter from the beginning. Though Satan's temptations are inevitable and common to all, he can't force you to do anything against your will. But he can tempt you in the hopes of getting you to make bad choices. That's what he did with Judas, who loved money and power. He ensnared Judas and had him choose to betray Jesus. Beware! The enemy works to ensnare you in similar ways.

Third, the Father in heaven had given Jesus all authority in heaven and on earth. The Son had come from him, and would soon return to him.

These lessons are ones you need to know well. But the most

important lesson—one that applies to all believers—is Jesus' call on your life to be a servant. Why did he take the towel and basin and began washing the disciples' feet? Luke's Gospel tells us. According to his telling of what happened that night, an argument had erupted among the disciples about who was the greatest (Luke 22:24-27). Sadly, this selfish debate exploded several times during their three-plus years together.

That's when Jesus took the towel and basin and started washing the disciples' feet. This domestic duty was usually reserved for a household helper. It was essential in a culture where people wore sandals and walked many miles on dusty or muddy roads, which would cause their feet to become exceedingly dirty.

Jesus himself had carried out a most menial household duty that only the lowest of servants would perform. He was showing humility—the earmark of anyone who would choose to follow him. He wanted all his followers to emulate his example.

You are called to wash others' feet. You are called to serve, not be served, and to give your life away to a dying world.

Do you acknowledge this truth today? If so, go find someone whose feet you can wash. Find someone you can serve. Find someone to whom you can give hope.

You will find yourself when you lose yourself in something greater than yourself. Your depression will lift like the noonday sun shining on creation.

It's one of the most important lessons you can ever learn.

✳ ✳

Daily Grace

Today's Reading: John 13:6-11

HEARING GOD'S VOICE FOR TODAY:
*"Jesus answered them, 'The one who has bathed does not need
to wash, except for his feet, but is completely clean. And you
are clean, but not every one of you.' For he knew who was to
betray him; that was why he said, 'Not all of you are clean.'"*

✳ ✳ ✳

There were two symbolic meanings behind the foot-washing Jesus
gave to the disciples. He wants all his followers to understand both
of them.

Peter objected when Jesus began to wash his feet. When Jesus told
Peter that he could not share in fellowship with him unless he washed
his feet, Peter asked Jesus to wash his entire body.

Peter's objection points to the first meaning: the forgiveness of your
sins. This was the purpose of the cross. When you accept the washing made available through the cross, you become "completely clean"
in God's eyes. All sins are forever forgiven and you become his for all
eternity. The only exception among the disciples was Judas, who had
already decided to betray Jesus. He was not one of our Lord's sheep.

There was another symbolic meaning behind the foot washing: Yes,
you are forever forgiven. But as you continue your life's journey, you
will still sin and accumulate dirt on your soul. You'll still fall prey to
your old nature's yearnings to rebel against the Lord. You'll still need
to return to him and ask for forgiveness.

John, in one of the letters he penned to the churches, wrote, "If you confess your sins, he is faithful and just and forgives you of all unrighteousness" (1 John 1:9).

In other words, even as God's child, you will need daily grace.

When you do something that hurts the Lord's heart, come back to the cross. Be washed again. Receive anew his steadfast love. It never ceases. It is new every morning.

Jesus loves to clean a sullied heart. He loves to renew a right spirit in us. He desires to give grace to the disobedient.

Jesus asks just one thing: Don't use his grace as an excuse to sin. That cheapens his grace. It makes a mockery of his death and resurrection. In doing this, you are taking advantage of his love as you rebel against him. It's a total misuse and abuse of his grace. It breaks his heart, and it deserves his severest condemnation.

Yes, following Jesus is costly. It's not for the fainthearted. It demands all you are to be all he is. It is extremely difficult and challenging at times.

But his grace is the fuel that will keep you moving forward. It will never fail you. It's what has empowerd you to live for Jesus until now. This grace will lead you home.

It should lead to a fervent faithfulness as you follow him.

Let Jesus wash you again and again with his grace—today, and every day.

✳ ✳

Forgiving Those Who Hurt You

Today's Reading: John 13:12-20

HEARING GOD'S VOICE FOR TODAY:
"I am not speaking of all of you; I know whom I have chosen. But the Scripture will be fulfilled, 'He who ate my bread has lifted his heel against me.'"

✳ ✳ ✳

Jesus was instructing his disciples about faithfulness. But he wanted them to realize that even though he had chosen all twelve of them, there was one who would not be faithful. He would betray Jesus. His name was Judas.

Have you ever been betrayed? Has someone hurt you deeply through lies, deceptions, and behind-the-scenes manipulations?

Most people have experienced this crucible. Some of them were great men of faith. For example, Moses faced a rebellion led by Korah. King David experienced betrayal on two different occasions by two different people. The first time was Ahithophel—a close friend and advisor. The second occurred through his son Absalom. The apostle Paul was betrayed by Alexander the Coppersmith and Demas.

It happened to Jesus as well. He wasn't surprised. Scripture had to be fulfilled (Psalm 41:9). But it still stung and scorched him. He loved Judas. He had made him treasurer over all money given to the disciples. This was not a small amount to oversee. Some widows gave significant money to fund Jesus' ministry. Judas had an important responsibility. Sadly, he failed the Lord.

Is there someone in your life who has betrayed and hurt you? If so, Jesus can empathize with the hurt in your heart. But you must not allow bitterness to eat away at your soul. It is a root that can defile you and many who live around you. It can choke away the Lord's grace and mercy.

If you cling to bitterness, you are the one eventually hurt the most. It's like drinking arsenic and expecting the other person to die. You repeatedly pay the price for another's sins against you. Sometimes this person is not even in your life anymore, and yet he continues to hurt you—even from the other side of the grave! That makes no sense.

You must forgive those who have hurt you. Refuse to hold a grudge so that the Father in heaven will forgive you. Release them to the Lord. Let him settle all debts and enact revenge. He knows all the details of what happened—much better than you do.

His justice is perfect.

If you persist in exacting revenge, Jesus will take his hands off the problem. It will become your deal. Or you can trust him and know that he will enact justice in the right way and time.

God has forgiven you a billion-dollar debt you owed him. Now forgive the person who owes you a ten-thousand-dollar debt. Let God settle the score.

In so doing, you are then released from the prison of your bitterness—and set free to live for the Lord.

✳ ✳

The Importance of Love and Humility

Today's Reading: John 13:21-30

HEARING GOD'S VOICE FOR TODAY:
*"One of his disciples, whom Jesus loved, was reclining
at table close to Jesus, so Simon Peter motioned to
him to ask Jesus of whom he was speaking."*

✳ ✳ ✳

Jesus and his disciples were celebrating the last supper. It was a sacred moment. The next day, Jesus would face the cross.

During the meal, he announced that one of them would betray him.

They were eating in a circle, reclining on their elbows around a table. Each person to the right of another had his head at the breast of the person to his left. This made it easy for an intimate conversation to occur between two people without others hearing it.

After Jesus announced he would be betrayed, Simon Peter motioned to the disciple next to Jesus—the one whose head was on the Lord's breast, to ask who would betray him.

Throughout the Gospel of John, this disciple is called the disciple "whom Jesus loved." He surely was. He was John, one of the sons of Zebedee, whom Jesus chose along with John's brother James. Together with Simon Peter, John was a member of Jesus' inner circle. His heart was devoted solely to the Lord. He desired, above all else, to do Jesus' will.

Would this describe you? Would Jesus call you a disciple whom he dearly loved?

That is his heart's desire. If you passionately love Jesus, it's most likely because you have discovered how much he first loved you. You love him in response to knowing how much he loves you and his willingness to give up his life for you.

Have you ever wondered why John always referred to himself as the disciple "whom Jesus loved" instead of using his actual name? Many believe it was because of his humility. He didn't desire his name to be closely attached to Jesus. He felt his readers would see it as self-promotional and prideful.

John wanted all attention and applause to be given to Jesus. He didn't want any glory for himself. He realized God crowns the humble with victory. He believed that humility precedes honor. He understood that the humility of a child is the way someone enters the kingdom of God. He knew that all glory belonged solely to the Lord.

Jesus loved John's unabashed love and humility.

Does your life emulate John's? Do you love Jesus as he did? Do you seek after humility? Do you know that everything you have in life comes from the Lord? Do you realize that true love for Jesus recognizes that before you ever loved him, he first loved you? Have you pondered recently the reality that he gave his life as an atoning sacrifice for your sin?

Love and humility are two major benchmarks that prove you belong to Jesus.

Pursue them both today—and all days.

* *

Love One Another

Today's Reading: John 13:31-35

HEARING GOD'S VOICE FOR TODAY:
"A new commandment I give to you, that you love one another: Just as I have loved you, you also are to love one another. By this all people will know that you are my disciples, if you have love for one another."

* * *

The cross was looming on the horizon. In just a few hours, Jesus would give his life for the salvation of the world.

Before going to the cross, the Lord wanted to give his disciples a profound teaching. It was a new commandment: As he had loved them, he now wanted them to love one another.

At first glance, this may not seem like a new commandment. Moses had told the Jews to love God with all their heart and their neighbors as themselves (Leviticus 19:18).

But Jesus' love was deeper and more powerful than Moses' words. "Just as I have loved you," he said. It would be evidenced by his death on a cross. It was an unconditional and self-sacrificial love. His would be a death that invited love for enemies and prayers for persecutors.

Jesus wanted his disciples to emulate the love displayed on the cross and show it to other people. When rightly done, this love would be a strong evangelistic tool. The world will know that you are one of Jesus' disciples by the way you love fellow believers.

The world knows little of this kind of love. Friends are willing to die for friends, but not enemies. People are willing to die for their country, but not for their persecutors.

The world's love is rooted in performance. It's often quid pro quo. What you do for me, I will do for you. You scratch my back, and I'll scratch yours. If you perform well, you receive plaudits and a raise. If not, you are on your own.

That's antithetical to God's kind of love. His love is unconditional and sacrificial. It's not rooted in merit. It lays down its life for friends and enemies alike. While you were still wallowing in your sin and headed toward eternal doom, Jesus came and died for you. He left the grandeur of heaven to enter the garbage of this world. He died a shameful, hideous death because of his love for you.

Jesus' followers are called to love one another the way he loves them. This ability to love others comes from God himself. Anyone who loves proves he's a child of God and knows God. But anyone who does not love does not know God, for God is love. Anyone who loves other followers of Jesus is living in the light and not causing others to stumble.

When Jesus' love is lived out rightly in his church, spiritual seekers will be drawn to him. They will desire to know this Savior whose love is not based on the exhausting demands of performance. They will want to be part of a group of people who love as he has loved them.

Everything else in this world will one day fade away. Three things never will: faith, hope, and love. And the greatest of these is love.

How he loves you!

Now love one another—even your enemies—the way he has loved you.

When you do, the world will know you truly belong to him.

Starting Over

Today's Reading: John 13:36-38

HEARING GOD'S VOICE FOR TODAY:
"Simon Peter said to him, 'Lord, where are you going?' Jesus answered him, 'Where I am going you cannot follow me now, but you will follow afterward.' Peter said to him, 'Lord, why can I not follow you now? I will lay down my life for you.' Jesus answered, 'Will you lay down your life for me? Truly, truly, I say to you, the rooster will not crow till you have denied me three times.'"

* * *

Jesus loved Simon Peter. He knew this disciple had a big heart for him. There was little question about Peter's devotion to the Lord.

But how Peter struggled with his flesh! He was so impetuous. Frequently he would speak before thinking. His emotions easily swayed him. That's why Jesus called him "Simon bar Jonah." In Scripture, "Jonah" is the same word for "dove." As a dove flies one direction and abruptly changes to another, so did Peter.

After Jesus' death and resurrection, Peter even fudged on the gospel of grace. He was in Antioch, eating with Gentiles—as he should have been. Then the Judaizers came to town. They were convinced that new believers needed to be under Jewish law and be circumcised, and they persuaded Peter of this. So he stopped having fellowship with Gentile converts.

Paul called out Peter publicly for his prejudice. Peter knew he was wrong and repented immediately.

Do you see the pattern? Even when you are filled with the Holy

Spirit, your flesh can still be easily manipulated. Often your spirit is willing, but your flesh is weak.

Peter asked Jesus where he was going. The Lord told Peter it was a place he couldn't immediately come to. Later, he would be able to. Jesus was referring to heaven. Peter said he wanted to follow the Lord now and would even be willing to die for him.

Once again, Peter was being impetuous. He didn't understand the profound disappointment he would feel after Jesus' death, nor the antagonism, hatred, fury, and persecution that he would receive from the religious authorities. Jesus foresaw the future. He knew that Peter would deny him three times.

Peter and Judas behaved similarly. Judas was tempted by power and money and failed Jesus. Peter was tempted by fear and cowardice and failed Jesus. Even though their sins were different, they both betrayed the Lord in his hour of greatest need.

Though they behaved similarly, their responses were very different. Judas never repented. He felt sorrow for what he had done, but he never repented. Instead, he committed suicide. By contrast, Peter felt sorrow and repented. And Jesus, in one of his resurrection appearances, assured Peter three times of his unconditional love and forgiveness for him—one for each of Peter's betrayals. Their relationship was restored.

Repentance is the key. It stops the behavior that is breaking God's heart. It admits you are wrong and chooses to go in a different direction. If you return to the Lord and repent of your wrong, he will restore you. He loves to heal wayward hearts and give second chances.

Failure happens only when you fail to return to Jesus. His grace covers all sins—no matter how great or small, including Peter's. Including yours.

You can't sin beyond his grace.

Choose Faith

Today's Reading: John 14:1-7

HEARING GOD'S VOICE FOR TODAY:
"Let not your hearts be troubled. Believe in God; believe also in me. In my Father's house are many rooms. If it were not so, would I have told you that I go to prepare a place for you?...I am the way, and the truth and the life. No one comes to the Father except through me."

✳ ✳ ✳

When difficulties come your way, don't let your heart be troubled. It's your choice whether to worry about a problem or not. You can choose to focus on either the size of your problems or the size of your God.

How can you stop worrying? Choose to believe in the Father. It's a command. He created and controls all. There's nothing he doesn't oversee. Everything you're worried about is under the heavenly Father's control and care. So why worry?

Believe also in the Son. Believe that he came from heaven to earth to die for your sins. Believe death is not the end for you. Believe that heaven is your home. Believe that nothing can separate you from Jesus' love. Believe he is stronger than your problems.

In the Father's house are many dwelling places, where you'll live forever. Jesus is now there, preparing a place for you. If this weren't true, why would he have told you? No falsehood can be uttered from his lips. You can trust what he says.

Jesus is *the* way to the Father. He alone grants access to him. There is no other name in heaven and on earth by which you can be saved.

Jesus is *the* truth. His teachings are true—including what he promised about eternal life. Unlike the enemy, who is the father of lies, Jesus cannot lie. Every word he speaks is truth because he is the truth.

Jesus is *the* life. Only he can confer eternal life on those who believe in him. It happens the moment you are birthed into his kingdom. He also gives you abundant life now.

Here is another of Jesus' "I am" statements in John's Gospel. Once again, he gives a clear claim to deity. It may be his most significant "I am" statement of all. It claims exclusivity for salvation.

Yes, that claim is offensive to some. But when people object to it, don't become defensive. Simply point them back to Jesus himself. It wasn't your idea. He made the claim, not you. They are offended with him, not you.

Difficulties will come. But don't let your heart be troubled. Rest peacefully in the Lord. He is a shelter for the oppressed, a refuge and fortress in times of trouble. Though troubles come, the Lord will rescue you each time. He is your hiding place; he is your strong arm each and every day you live. He is close to those who trust him.

Choose to have faith in the heavenly Father and the Son. Believe that your earthly troubles won't last very long and are producing a heavenly glory that far outweighs anything you are facing today.

With Jesus' help, you can persevere. And you can be certain your heavenly home is secure.

Jesus wouldn't lie to you about something so important.

Greater Works

Today's Reading: John 14:8-14

HEARING GOD'S VOICE FOR TODAY:
*"Believe me that I am in the Father and the Father is in me, or else
believe on account of the works themselves. Truly, truly, I say to you,
whoever believes in me will also do the works that I do and greater
works than these will he do, because I am going to the Father."*

✳ ✳ ✳

Jesus told his disciples that he is in the Father, and the Father is in him.
This is an astounding claim, a spiritual mystery. The finite human
mind cannot grasp it. But it's true.

There is a mutual indwelling presence of the Father in the Son, and
vice versa. They are in union with one another. It's a perfect love relationship. Yet along with the Holy Spirit, they are three distinct per-
sonalities. They comprise one God in three persons—a blessed Trinity.

You aren't expected to understand this. Thoughtful, intelligent people through the ages have tried to explain the Trinity. But they can't.
All human attempts are inadequate. Would you want to trust a God
whom you could easily explain?

Jesus then told his disciples that if they struggled to believe what he
said, they could look at his works and amazing miracles. Who else but
God could do such signs and wonders?

Finally, Jesus told them that they would be able to accomplish
greater works than these.

What does this mean? When the Holy Spirit came upon them, his
presence indwelt them permanently. Jesus' word, works, and power
would no longer be limited to his physical presence in a specific place.

Rather, his followers everywhere would be able to do evangelism, teach about his kingdom, do deeds of compassion, pray for the sick, and see healings occur and the demonic flee.

Through the centuries, the number of Jesus' followers has grown and their influence continues to expand. Lives, cultures, and societies are being transformed. His kingdom is advancing around the globe— all for his glory.

Have you done any of his works today? Have you shown his forgiveness to anyone? Have you shared his eternal truths? Have you prayed for someone and seen his miraculous power? Have you been an instrument for changing someone's eternal trajectory? Have you offered a compassionate hand to a hurting person?

Those are among the reasons why Jesus created you. He wants you to be an instrument of his peace. He wants his power to flow through you to a dying world. He desires for you to invest your life in other people's lives.

Open your heart, and let him fill you with his love. Then go to where he tells you to go, and give his love away. Work with enthusiasm, as though you are working for the Lord and not for people. He will reward you for all the good you do.

And he will do greater works through you than you could ever possibly imagine.

Another Helper

Today's Reading: John 14:15-17

HEARING GOD'S VOICE FOR TODAY:
"If you love me, you will keep my commandments. And I will ask the Father, and he will give you another Helper, to be with you forever."

✳ ✳ ✳

True love always manifests itself in willing obedience. If you love your spouse, you will serve him or her. A marriage in which the spouse expresses love but never does what is right in marriage is living a lie.

And what is love? Love is not only an emotion; it's emotion in motion. It's a verb. It acts, gives, shares, and cares.

Jesus said that if you love him, you will obey his commandments. Obedience proves your love for him. It's a very simple teaching.

While Jesus was with his disciples, he made an extraordinary promise for all his followers, including you. He said that he would ask the Father to send them "another Helper." This "Helper" is the Holy Spirit. He is Jesus' very presence.

Jesus promised the Spirit because he knew you would need every heavenly power, assistance, and resource available to face your daily trials. Inwardly, he will encourage you, and give you comfort, and help keep you moving forward in life.

The Helper will always encourage you. He will always remind you of your identity in Christ, and that your sins are forgiven. He is your defense attorney and he will refute any bogus charges and accusations made against you by the enemy.

The Helper is Jesus' divine presence with and in you. He is with you always—even to the close of the age. He will give you the power to be Christ's witness both locally and globally. He who lives in you is greater than the enemy who lives in the world.

Don't fear when you are speaking to another person about Jesus—whether a peasant or a prince, a commoner or a king. The Helper will give you the words to speak when you need to speak them. Even if you are brought before people who are hostile toward him, you will never need to worry about what to say or how to defend yourself. The Helper will teach you at that time what to say.

When you believe, the Holy Spirit is placed within you so that you will be able to obey God's decrees. He will teach you what is true. And he will empower you to face any mountain and see it dissolve into the depths of the sea.

Don't be afraid, for the Lord is with you. God's personal, powerful presence through the Holy Spirit will allow you not to fear, for he is your God. He will strengthen you and uphold you with his righteous right hand.

Even though you may walk through the valley of the shadow of death, he will be with you.

The Lord of hosts, the one who commands all the angel armies, is by your side.

And always remember: Jesus plus you equals all the powers in heaven are now at your disposal.

✳ ✳

Your Heart: God's Home

Today's Reading: John 14:18-24

HEARING GOD'S VOICE FOR TODAY:
*"Jesus answered him, 'If anyone loves me, he will keep my
word, and my Father will love him, and we will come
to him and make our home with him. Whoever does
not love me does not keep my words. And the word that
you hear is not mine but the Father's who sent me.'"*

✳ ✳ ✳

Once again, we see Jesus saying that if you love him, you will respond by obeying his commandments. He said that obedience to him will bring a personal manifestation of his presence to you.

Jesus' half brother, Jude, asked why the Lord would manifest himself to the disciples and not the world. The answer was simple. He couldn't. This manifestation was for those who loved and obeyed him. This obedience proves love for him. The world doesn't desire this. It's anathema to the spiritual skeptic.

When you love and obey Jesus, both the Father and the Son come to make a home with you. And though they live in your heart, there are times when they feel as if they aren't welcome. There are things in your heart that are inconsistent with their presence in you.

Is your heart truly their home? Do you give them total access to every one of your life's rooms? Are there any rooms you won't allow them to enter?

Is your life's den littered with unholy literature and waste? Are there programs on your television, computer, or social media that would cause you to be embarrassed if they watched them with you?

Why would you watch anything that you knew Jesus and the Father wouldn't want you to watch?

Will you allow them to oversee your kitchen—watching your diet to make sure you eat correctly so your body remains healthy? To make sure you drink lots of water and not ingest too much alcohol, sugar, and bad carbohydrates?

How about the exercise room? Will you meet them there to exercise your body? If you remain sedentary, it will affect your spirit and soul. They are undeniably connected. If one part is neglected, other parts will be as well. Do you manage your body well, remembering the Holy Spirit indwells it?

How about your bedroom? The one sleeping with you is your spouse to whom you're committed forever in marriage, correct? You do know that's God's original design and will, don't you? Also, are you getting enough sleep to remain healthy? Are you burning the candle at both ends? If so, you are not as bright as you think you are. Physically healthy people need sleep. And they know that during their sleep the Lord will oversee them, give them his peace, and renew their bodies and spirits.

The Father and the Son will feel welcome in your heart when you love and obey their words.

And if you love them, you will give them complete access to every room. No part of your heart is denied access.

Your heart will be their home.

Has this happened?

✳ ✳

Read God's Word with Confidence

Today's Reading: John 14:25-26

HEARING GOD'S VOICE FOR TODAY:
*"These things I have spoken to you while I am still with
you. But the Helper, the Holy Spirit, whom the Father
will send in my name, he will teach you all things and
bring to your remembrance all that I have said to you."*

✳ ✳ ✳

The teachings Jesus gave to his disciples in John 13–17 comprise
what is commonly called the Upper Room Discourse. They are
among the most intimate insights he shared with them. He wanted
these truths to be indelibly etched in their minds.

Here, Jesus promised them again that the Helper, the third person
of the Godhead, would be sent to them in his name. He would ask the
Helper to come, and the Helper would respond without hesitation.

Note that Jesus called the Helper "he." That's because he is a person. When he indwells you, you have a personal, living, and dynamic
relationship with him. Because the Helper lives in you, his very nature
is within you.

But don't miss the great work the Holy Spirit did through his disciples in the writings of the New Testament—God's Word. Jesus said
that the Helper would bring to their minds all his teachings. Their
written words about his life in the Gospels and instructions to the
churches about right doctrine and practice would be his very words
written through them.

This work of the Holy Spirit allows us to have confidence in the
words of the New Testament. The words written by the disciples were

supernatural— their words were actually God's words. Their insights were actually God's insights.

What the disciples wrote down was not guesswork. It wasn't from human hearts. All the words of the New Testament are God-breathed. The disciples' written words were Jesus' words. That makes them reliable, authoritative, and accurate.

You can trust the Bible. It's not mere human opinion. It's not from a group of people who wrote down mere subjective thoughts. It's God's authoritative Word.

Through the ages, the Helper guided prophets and apostles to write down exactly what the Father willed them to say. They were not mere spiritual stenographers, but real men, in real times, listening to and being led by the Helper to pen the Father's heart.

The fact they were chosen by the Father to write down his words gives those words complete authority. The Helper guided them in this work.

The Bible is God's Word—guided and overseen by the Helper, the Holy Spirit, the silent sovereign, and the third person of the Trinity.

Read the Word with confidence. The grass withers and the flowers fade, but the Word of God stands forever.[6] Heaven and earth will disappear, but Jesus' words will never disappear.[7] It gives hope and encouragement. It prospers wherever it is sent, read, believed, and obeyed.

Believe that its promises are true.

✳ ✳

The Gift of Peace

Today's Reading: John 14:27-31

HEARING GOD'S VOICE FOR TODAY:
*"Peace I leave with you, my peace I give to you. Not as the
world gives to you…For the Father is greater than I."*

✳ ✳ ✳

Jesus wants to give you the gift of his peace. The Hebrew word translated "peace" is *shalom*. It's a much richer word than the English
word *peace*.

The English word suggests an absence of conflict, turmoil, and trials. By contrast, *shalom* means positive blessing—especially in terms of
a relationship with the Father. It's the sense that all is well. Everything
in your life is working as designed.

That's the kind of peace Jesus wants you to experience. You are able
to rejoice because you know the Father is working through the trials
you face. You know that tribulation is bringing about perseverance,
and perseverance proven character, and proven character hope. This
hope never disappoints because it knows the Holy Spirit is pouring out
God's love inside your heart.[8]

Shalom is what Jesus desires to give to you. The world can't give it.
It tries to give peace—the absence of conflict—but has never been suc-
cessful. There are always hot spots around the globe that cause tensions.
There always will be until Jesus returns.

Jesus' peace is his personal, abiding presence—no matter what is
surrounding you.

Jesus also said that the Father is greater than him. That does not mean that he has more power and authority. It does not mean that Jesus is inferior to the Father in any way.

Rather, it means that Jesus willingly submitted his power and authority to the Father's request that he come to earth and die on a cross to save the lost. During the Savior's thirty-plus years on earth, he gladly and willingly submitted his will to the Father's.

Jesus did not think of equality with the Father as something to be grasped. He put on human flesh in the form of a servant. He humbled myself in obedience to the point of death on the cross. While on earth, he submitted to the Father's authority. It was his joy to do so.

The Son did all this for love. He gave up his power and position in heaven to save you. He wanted to show you the nature of the Father. In the Old Testament, people heard about him. In the New Testament, they saw him. The Old Testament is like radio. The New Testament is like television.

At one time, people only heard about the Father. But through Jesus, they could see the Father face to face.

Jesus came to give you *shalom*. Receive it today. It's what will allow you to lie down and sleep peacefully, knowing the Lord will keep you safe. His peace brings quietness and confidence of soul. It flows like a gentle river, and guards your heart and mind as you rest in him.

This peace is available to all God's children. It eliminates fear. It causes trouble to melt before it. It surpasses all understanding.

The world can't give it to you.

His presence will.

✳ ✳

Created to Bear Fruit for God

Today's Reading: John 15:1-11

HEARING GOD'S VOICE FOR TODAY:
*"I am the true vine, and my Father is the vinedresser. Every branch
in me that does not bear fruit he takes away, and every branch that
does bear fruit he prunes that it may bear more fruit...I am the
vine; you are the branches. Whoever abides in me and I in him, he
it is that bears much fruit, for apart from me you can do nothing."*

✳ ✳ ✳

This is the last of Jesus' seven "I am" statements in John's Gospel. Once again, it points to his deity.

He said, "I am the true vine." The word "true" contrasts him with Israel. The term "vine," or "vineyard," was used in Old Testament nomenclature as a symbol of Israel. But Israel failed to produce fruit for the Father and be a light to the nations.

That is why Jesus is the true vine. As his followers abide in him, they will succeed where Israel failed. Through them, the gospel will spread throughout the world.

The Father in heaven is the vinedresser. His work in you ensures fruitfulness. This happens when he connects you, the branches, with Jesus, the vine. What connects you is your faith. That's why the Lord desires great faith. When you are solidly one with him, his life will easily flow to you. Who he is becomes who you are. And with him, you can do anything.

As the vinedresser, the Father sometimes must prune branches. It can be painful, but it's very purposeful. He does this so you will bear more fruit.

The Father prunes you. He sees certain things in your life that are preventing full fruitfulness and must be removed. Thus, the painful process of pruning begins.

Perhaps you are experiencing that right now. Something in your life has been removed that you thought was important. You're wondering what the Father is doing.

As this pruning takes place, try to look at it from the Father's perspective. He knows you well. He realizes what is keeping your full growth in him from happening. Trust him in the pruning. Though it's painful, remember that he is an expert vinedresser. He knows what he's doing.

And remain solidly connected to Jesus. Then the fruit of the Spirit will be produced in your character: love, joy, peace, patience, kindness, faithfulness, gentleness, and self-control. Then who you are will be reproduced in the lives of others. Remember: You reproduce who you are and not what you do. This brings much glory and praise to God.

The Lord created you to bear great fruit for him—both inwardly and outwardly. You should be like a tree on a riverbank, bearing fruit each season for him. Even in old age, you are to remain vital for the Lord and produce fruit for his glory. That's why you were placed on this planet: For his life to be in you and to flow through you so that you bear much fruit for him.

Don't be dismayed when pruning takes place. The Father is removing some good and bad fruit so you can produce more and better fruit. Just make sure you remain connected to the vine.

You were created to bear great fruit for God.

Jesus is the true vine. Remain in him.

Apart from him, you can do nothing.

✳ ✳

Jesus Is Your Friend

Today's Reading: John 15:12-17

HEARING GOD'S VOICE FOR TODAY:

*"These things I have spoken to you, that my joy may be
in you, and that your joy may be full...Greater love has
no one than this, that someone lay down his life for his
friends...No longer do I call you servants, for the servant
does not know what his master is doing; but I have called
you friends. You did not choose me, but I chose you."*

✳ ✳ ✳

Jesus wants you to have his complete joy. It comes by abiding in him.
When your life is rooted in him, his joy will be in you. This reality
can't be forced or mandated. It naturally flows from him to you when
you abide and remain in him.

The Savior wants you to know he loves you. The proof is that he laid
down his life for you. It's the greatest example of selfless love the world
has ever seen. He laid down his life for his frends.

You are his friend. Moses and Abraham were also called his friends.
Yes, before you gave your life to the Lord, you were a rebel and an
enemy. But now, through Jesus' death, you are a close friend. He will
never betray or desert you. You are friends forever.

What a friend you have in Jesus! He bears all your sins and grief. You
have the privilege of coming to him daily in prayer. You forfeit a lot
of peace and bear much needless pain because you don't go to him in
prayer. So carry everything to him in prayer. After all, he is your friend.

Here is another insight about your relationship with Jesus. You are
no longer merely a servant. Humanly speaking, servants have no rights

or relationship with their master. They are second-class citizens. Their job description is simply to obey the master.

But as a believer, you are an adopted child of the King of the universe. All he owns is now yours. Royal blood pulsates through your veins. The Father yearns to spend time with you.

Yes, you still obey him—as a servant does. But there is a major shift in motivation. You obey because you *want* to, not because you *have* to. You obey because of your close relationship with him. Joy increases as you willingly obey what he tells you to do.

You are Jesus' personal friend, and a chosen member of his heavenly family. He wants to spend time with you every day, as any good friend wants to do. He is closer than a brother. Your friendship with him will never be broken. He died so you could be friends. Could there be greater love? What more could he give to you?

Live today in the reality of that close, personal relationship.

It should bring joy to your heart. And make his joy in you complete.

✳ ✳

The Proof of Faithfulness

Today's Reading: John 15:18-25

HEARING GOD'S VOICE FOR TODAY:
"If the world hates you, know that it has hated me before
it hated you...I chose you out of the world, therefore
the world hates you...A servant is not greater than his
master. If they persecuted me, they will also persecute
you...Whoever hates me hates my Father also."

✳ ✳ ✳

If you are a faithful follower of Jesus, the world will hate you. Don't be surprised when that happens. It first hated him.

Why does the world hate him? There are several reasons.

First, Jesus' life exposes human pride. It shows how we trust in our own insights and ways. It shows self-exaltation and worship of self. It proves we want the world to revolve around us so that we get all the fame and glory. By contrast, his followers want only God to receive the glory.

Second, we want to control our own life. We want to oversee all the shots and yield control to no one. But the Lord calls us to yield control of our life and trust him. He tells us that if we try to save our life, we will lose it. But if we give up our life for his sake and the sake of the gospel, we will gain it.

Third, we want to earn our own salvation. We think we are good enough to enter heaven, but we aren't. Jesus says that all fall far short of the glory of God. We need a Savior who will save us by grace, not our works. Only he can make this possible. We are offended when we hear that salvation is by his grace alone.

Jesus chose you out of the world to follow him. That means you are to reject the world's values. You now belong to him and possess his kingdom values. They are completely different than the world's values. The way you live for Jesus should remind people of their rebellion against him. As you live for him, the world will hate you as it hated him.

The servant is not greater than the master, nor is the pupil greater than the teacher, nor is the disciple greater than the mentor. If it happened to Jesus, it will happen to you. If people hate the word of truth, the world will hate it when you speak and live it.

When people hate you, don't retaliate or seek revenge. Leave those individuals to heaven. The Lord will rightly deal with them when the time is right.

You may feel lonely at times. Don't despair. Jesus will be with you wherever you may go. Even when you go through deep waters, he will be there with you. Don't ever be shaken. Call upon the Lord and he will whisper to you, "I am right here."

Yes, Jesus chose you from the world. Nevertheless, he calls you back into the world. You are to be in the world, but not of it.

You are Jesus' light in a dark world. Shine brightly for his glory!

You are Jesus' salt in a decaying world. Be very salty!

You are Jesus' ambassador to the world. Represent him well!

And don't be surprised when the hatred comes.

It shows you're being effective for your Lord.

A Faithful Witness

Today's Reading: John 15:26-27

HEARING GOD'S VOICE FOR TODAY:
*"But when the Helper comes, whom I will send to you from the
Father, the Spirit of truth, who proceeds from the Father, he
will bear witness about me. And you also will bear witness,
because you have been with me from the beginning."*

* * *

Jesus promised his disciples that the Holy Spirit would come to them. He would infuse in them a power from heaven. His life would live in and through them.

The Holy Spirit's purpose is to bear witness to Jesus. He wants no public attention or acclaim for himself. He is the silent sovereign.

Note the concept of the Trinity here in John 15:26-27. Though the term *Trinity* never appears in the Bible, the idea is clearly seen. The Holy Spirit flows from the Father, at Jesus' command, to bear witness to the Son. There is one God in three persons: Father, Son, and Holy Spirit. There are not three gods in Christian orthodoxy.

The Trinity is a profound mystery. It can't be explained by human logic. But it's clearly taught and seen in the Word. For example, Jesus told his disciples to baptize in the name of the Father, the Son, and the Holy Spirit.[9]

The Holy Spirit wants to bear witness to Jesus. He desires that his name be exalted above all other names.

When the Spirit enters your life, you desire to yield to his guidance. His heart becomes your heart and you are motivated to bear witness for Jesus as well.

At Pentecost, that's exactly what happened. When the Holy Spirit filled the 120 who were gathered in the Upper Room, they were consumed with a desire to witness to those who had gathered in Jerusalem from many nations. They flooded the streets to share the good news. They were so joyful that some observers thought them to be intoxicated in the early morning hours.

Jesus told the disciples that when the Holy Spirit came upon them, they'd be his witnesses—both locally and globally. A major evidence of the infilling of the Spirit in your life is your bold and confident witness about the Lord—both locally and globally.

Do you desire to witness for Jesus? Or are you still trying to please people? Are you more concerned about your reputation than his? Are you concerned your name will be rejected rather than his name exalted?

You can't have it both ways. You can't be Jesus' follower and say you're filled with the Holy Spirit and not be a bold witness for him. In fact, the word "witness," in the original Greek text, is *martus*—the word from which we get the English word *martyr*.

If you are a witness for Jesus, you are willing to give your life for the Lord's cause. You are faithful until the end of this life. You cannot deny the reality of what Jesus has done in you. You know he has begun a good work in you and you're certain he will be faithful to complete it, even if you are called to be a martyr.

Is this you?

Are you a faithful witness?

✳ ✳

The Work of the Holy Spirit

Today's Reading: John 16:1-11

HEARING GOD'S VOICE FOR TODAY:
*"When he comes, he will convict the world concerning sin
and righteousness and judgment: concerning sin, because
they do not believe in me; concerning righteousness, because
I go to the Father, and you will see me no longer; concerning
judgment, because the ruler of this world is judged."*

✳ ✳ ✳

Here, Jesus has much to say to us about the promised Helper. When he comes, he will do three necessary works that will point people toward faith in him. What are they?

First, he will convict people of their sin. This is the important first step that's necessary for someone to come to faith. Most people believe they are basically good and occasionally do bad things. The opposite is true. They are basically selfish and occasionally do good things. And they need to realize that the wages of sin is death. The Helper will convict them of this essential truth and their need for a Savior.

Second, he will convict people of their unrighteousness. Perfect obedience to God's moral law, the Ten Commandments, is God's standard for salvation. Yet no one can ever achieve it. No one is righteous, not one. All people fall far short of God's glory. Once this conviction occurs from the Helper, they will realize their need for a Savior.

Third, he will convict people of the reality of the final judgment. This teaching is unpopular. People prefer to believe that life is only about eating, drinking, and being merry—for tomorrow you may die. They think that God is an eternal granddaddy who, after death, will merely wink at them, pat them on the head, and say, "There, there, it'll all be okay."

The Helper will contradict this lie. He will convict people that one day they will face their Maker and be held accountable for how they lived. He will remind them that a future, eternal judgment is coming. Jesus will be the Judge of the living and the dead. By revealing this truth, the Helper will show people their need for a Savior.

No one will come to Jesus for salvation unless they are convicted by the Holy Spirit of their sin, unrighteousness, and the reality of a final judgment. People will love him in direct proportion to how great a sinner they know they are. Until the Helper convicts them of these realities, they will never feel a need for a Savior. No one will move toward faith.

But if you have not received Jesus as your Savior, you are a sinner who has missed God's mark for your life. You are a rebel who has fought against his kingdom rule. You are ungodly, seeking your own selfish way. You deserve eternal separation from him, with hell being your eternal destiny.

Has the Helper convicted your heart of these awful realities? If so, here is some good news.

Jesus personally carried your sins in his body on the cross so that you can be dead to sin and live for what is right. Once you've confessed your sins to him, he will forgive you of all unrighteousness and you will possess a personal relationship with him. Your eternal trajectory will have changed.

Heaven is your eternal home.

And you now know how amazing God's grace truly is.

✳ ✳

The Spirit of Truth

Today's Reading: John 16:12-15

Hearing God's Voice for Today:
*"When the Spirit of truth comes, he will guide you into all
the truth, for he will not speak on his own authority, but
whatever he hears he will speak, and he will declare to
you the things that are to come. He will glorify me, for
he will take what is mine and declare it to you."*

✳ ✳ ✳

Jesus' greatest gift to you is not earthly presents but his eternal presence. He promised he would be with you—even to the close of the age. That promise is fulfilled when, at the moment of salvation, the Spirit of truth comes to you.

Notice Jesus called him the Spirit of truth. He wants to guide you into all truth. There is absolute truth in the world; the Father ordered it that way.

Jesus is that truth.

If you are truly seeking him with all your heart, you will be guided into all truth. You will deny the lie of this world that truth is whatever you believe it to be or that truth is a social construct. Rather, you will understand the difference between right and wrong and be able to discern good from evil. Absolute truth will form the foundation of your faith.

The Spirit of truth does not speak on his own authority. He hears from Jesus, and Jesus speaks through him. The Spirit only speaks what Jesus tells him.

The Helper does not want any attention. He wishes to point people to Jesus and for him alone to be exalted. He yearns for you to see that Jesus is the King of kings. He longs for you to believe that one day, every knee will bow and every tongue will confess that Jesus is Lord.

The Holy Spirit knows the future and how the world will end. He reveals insights about future events—especially Jesus' second coming—through the Word. Though you should never attempt to predict the time or date of Christ's return, you are told to look at the times and seasons and discern how they fit with his revelations.

The Helper not only knows the world's future, but also discerns your future. He is aware of where your life is headed. Perhaps he will reveal it to you.

Most often, though, he will not.

Nothing in your life is catching the Helper by surprise. He will guide you with every step you take. You do not need to worry about tomorrow, for tomorrow will bring its own worries. Today's troubles are enough for today. The Holy Spirit is guiding you along the right path and is watching over every step you take. You can be sure his plans for you are good.

Do you need truth today? Seek the Holy Spirit of truth. He will reveal it to you.

Do you want to glorify Jesus with all your words and works? That is the Helper's desire as well. Seek the Holy Spirit of truth. He will show you how to glorify Jesus.

The Spirit's presence and guidance is Jesus' greatest gift to you.

Rest peacefully and securely today in him.

✳ ✳

Your Sorrow Turned to Joy

Today's Reading: John 16:16-24

HEARING GOD'S VOICE FOR TODAY:

*"You will weep and lament, but the world will rejoice. You will
be sorrowful, but your sorrow will turn to joy. When a woman
is giving birth, she has sorrow because her hour has come, but
when she has delivered the baby, she no longer remembers the
anguish, for joy that a human being has been born into the
world...Ask, you will receive, that your joy may be full."*

✳ ✳ ✳

Jesus knew that after the cross, his followers would be forlorn, weep,
and lament. Conversely, the world would rejoice over his demise.

But Jesus also knew that his followers' sadness wouldn't last forever.
He wanted them to know their sorrow would eventually change to joy.

Jesus used contrasts to teach us. How can we know joy without sadness? Or how can we know happiness without heartache? It's one way
he is able to take that which is evil and use it for good.

Jesus then gave his disciples an illustration to make his point—he
referred to an event that happens daily. He asked them to remember
what happens in childbirth.

When a mother is delivering her baby, the pain is excruciating. It
increases with each contraction as the hour of delivery approaches. Her
sorrow becomes increasingly greater.

But after the baby is delivered and is placed on her chest, the pain
is forgotten and she is overcome with joy.

That was what happened with the disciples. They knew great pain after the cross and thought they had no hope. Their sorrow increased with every passing hour.

Jesus then appeared to them in his resurrection body. When they realized he was alive, their sorrow was immediately transformed into joy. New life and hope pulsated in their veins. Their joy became their strength.

You may think that your present situation is hopeless. The mountain before you appears too steep to be climbed. Sorrow fills your heart as you face the seemingly impossible.

Don't be discouraged. Don't give up. The Father is able to make lemonade out of your lemons. He can take your dramas and give daylight. He is able to do exceedingly and abundantly more than you could ever hope for or imagine. During your time of discouragement, remember a mother giving birth to her child. Your child is coming. Your deliverance is just around the corner.

Persevere in your prayers. Remember how Jesus has answered you in the past. When you ask and you receive an answer, joy fills your heart. Sorrow is immediately turned to joy. In him your heart rejoices, for you trust in his name. You may plant in tears, but your harvest will come with shouts of joy. You may weep as you plant the seed, but you will sing as you return with the harvest. Therefore, be overwhelmed with joy in the Lord your God. Rejoice in the Lord always. Let me say it again: Rejoice![10]

He will keep you from falling away and will bring you with great joy into his glorious presence without a single fault.[11]

Jesus' plans for you are good. He will use your sorrow for good.

It's always darkest before dawn.

Your joy will come in the morning.

✳ ✳

You Are an Overcomer

Today's Reading: John 16:26-33

HEARING GOD'S VOICE FOR TODAY:
*"Do you now believe? Behold, the hour is coming, indeed
it has come, when you will be scattered, each to his own
home, and will leave me alone. Yet I am not alone, for
the Father is with me. I have said these things to you, that
in me you may have peace. In the world you will have
tribulation. But take heart; I have overcome the world."*

✳ ✳ ✳

The hour had come for the fulfillment of the prophecy in Zechariah 13:7. The sheep were scattered, and the shepherd left alone. But Jesus knew he could face this ordeal because his Father in heaven was with him.

Jesus, based on his own experiences, was able to assure that you'd have peace—the abiding feeling that all is well with your soul—regardless of the circumstances surrounding you.

He told his disciples that in this world, they would experience tribulation. Not one is immune. There are no exemptions.

Jesus doesn't want anyone to think that if they follow him they will never experience trials, conflicts, difficulties, or challenges. Nothing could be farther from the truth. Rain falls on the just and the unjust alike. His followers must share in his sufferings.

In fact, you are warned that trials will increase when you follow Jesus. How can this be?

First, because you are a follower, the enemy will target you more viciously. You are a threat to the enemy's kingdom of darkness. He will increase and intensify his temptations and attacks upon your soul.

Second, the world will hate you. It hated Jesus; it will hate you as well. Your kingdom values now stand contrary to what the world holds dear. The world despises Jesus' message. Consequently, it will try to hurt the messenger.

Third, you will experience more intense battles with your flesh. The flesh is your fallen human nature. It yearns for self to be exalted above all. When the Spirit resides in you, the flesh and Spirit are contrary to one another. The more influential the Spirit becomes, the greater the pushback from the flesh. The crucifixion of your flesh becomes a daily battle where you must choose who sits on the throne of your heart: flesh or the Spirit.

But don't forget: Jesus said he has overcome the world. You can too. So take heart. Be filled with courage. The Spirit in you is greater than he who lives in the world.

Jesus stands victorious over all the powers of the world, the flesh, and the devil. All have been defeated by his resurrection. And as a believer, that power now lives in you. His strength in you will enable you to overcome all things.

Because he lives, you can face anything. Because he lives, all fear is gone. Because he was victorious, you can be too. Your present, temporary troubles are light and small in comparison to the glory that awaits you. It will greatly outweigh what you've gone through. Plus, it will last forever.

You are now more than a conqueror through him who loves you.

Live today in that victorious and conquering power.

The Glory of Jesus

Today's Reading: John 17:1-5

HEARING GOD'S VOICE FOR TODAY:

*"Father, the hour has come; glorify your Son that the Son
may glorify you, since you have given him authority over
all flesh, to give eternal life to all whom you have given
him. And this is eternal life, that they know you the only true
God, and Jesus Christ whom you have sent. I glorified you
on earth, having accomplished the work that you gave me to
do. And now, Father, glorify me in your own presence with
the glory that I had with you before the world existed."*

* * *

This is the beginning of Jesus' final prayer for his disciples. Prayer
wasn't an afterthought for him. It was his lifeline to the Father. It's
what gave him strength and power. It should be the same with you.

The hour had arrived for the Son to accomplish the work for which
he'd been sent: To die for the forgiveness of our sins and give us eternal life.

Jesus knew the Father would be glorified by his death on the cross.
God's perfect love and justice are intermixed. His holiness was satisfied by his wrath being poured out on Jesus, and not you. His love was
shown by the free gift of the forgiveness of your sins.

Note that Jesus asked the Father to glorify him in his presence.
How was this done? It happened when, after Jesus' death on the cross,
where for a while he was separated from his sinless Father because all
our sin rested on him, both the Father and the Son were restored to

perfect union in heaven—a union that existed in all eternity before Jesus came to earth.

Your greatest need is now met: The forgiveness of your sins. You now possess the gift of eternal life. You know the one true God through the one the Father sent to you to give you the gift of eternal life—Jesus. What Adam lost in the Garden of Eden, Jesus restored. Humanity has union life with God.

The Lord Jesus Christ accomplished the work the Father sent him to do. When he cried out on the cross with his last breath, "It is finished," his work was done. He obeyed perfectly the righteous requirements of the moral law, the Ten Commandments.

Where you failed, Jesus succeeded. Your disobedience brought you judgment. His obedience brought you forgiveness.

The judgment due you fell upon him. Jesus, who knew no sin, became sin so that you might become the righteousness of God. If you have accepted Christ as Savior, the Father now accepts you. He sees only his forgiveness and his righteousness in your heart.

Jesus is now with the Father again. It's the place where he pre-existed with him before the world was ever created. Today Jesus sits at the Father's right hand, waiting for the time when the Father tells him to return and judge the living and the dead. His glorification is complete.

The Lord is compassionate and merciful, slow to get angry and filled with an unfailing love. He forgives every kind of sin and rebellion. He lavishes love to the thousandth generation for those who love him. He redeems you from death and crowns you with his tender mercies.

How great is the Father's love for you, that he would make you his child. Abide in his love. It's the most powerful force in the universe.

It's what brought Jesus from heaven to earth to you.

It's what will take you home one day.

✳ ✳

Jesus Is Praying for You

Today's Reading: John 17:6-10

HEARING GOD'S VOICE FOR TODAY:
"I am praying for them. I am not praying for the world but for those whom you have given me, for they are yours. All mine are yours, and yours are mine, and I am glorified in them."

✳ ✳ ✳

Here, Jesus gives you a powerful promise from his heart to yours. It should give you great comfort and hope.

What is that promise? He is praying for you and your needs right now.

This is not a promise for those who don't believe in him and don't claim the power of his name. He is not praying for them.

But for those who know him and have received his gift of forgiveness, he is constantly praying for them before the Father. What you ask, in his name, he takes to the Father. He hears every one of your prayers and responds according to his perfect will. He knows every single need you have even before you present it to him.

What should you do if you don't know how to pray and what to ask for? The Spirit understands your heart. He will rightly interpret your needs.

He will then express your needs to the Father. Indeed, the Spirit and the Son are both making intercession for you. That should lift your heart when you feel overwhelmed and don't know how to pray.

Don't let your heart be troubled. Don't fear. Don't fret over evildoers. Don't be anxious about anything. Can your worries add even a single moment to your life? Can they add an inch to your height? Worry dominates the lives of those who don't believe in the Lord.

Rather, take courage. There is something you can do to address your problems.

What is it? Come to Jesus in prayer. He already knows all your needs. Make your requests known to him and sprinkle them with thanksgiving. Be thankful for all he has given to you. Remember and be thankful for previously answered prayers. Make a list if you need to.

Give all your cares to the Lord, for he cares about you. Let him carry them. He is able to do so. Experience the peace that passes understanding. It's given to you through Jesus—the one who is carrying your load, the one who takes your prayers to the Father.

He might answer yes. Or maybe you'll need to wait. Perhaps God has a better plan. What appears to be a *no* is God's perfect, sovereign care for you.

But he will respond. He hears and answers every request made to him.

Trust him.

Know that the response will be enveloped in perfect love.

And one day, you will understand his perfect answer.

✳ ✳

Jesus Prays a Specific Prayer for You

Today's Reading: John 17:15-16

HEARING GOD'S VOICE FOR TODAY:
"I do not ask that you take them out of the world, but that you keep them from the evil one."

✳ ✳ ✳

Here, Jesus continues in his prayers for his disciples—and this includes you.

His prayer is that you will never withdraw from the fallen world in which you live. At times, you may want to. But it is better that you don't.

God's will for your life is that you remain in the world. You are to try to influence it for good. You are to point people to Jesus and advance his kingdom on earth.

You are salt and light in the world. Salt is effective only if it's out of the saltshaker. When placed in meat, it gives taste and serves as a preservative. Likewise, light is effective only when it's shone into darkness. Then it can show people the next steps by which they can move forward.

Jesus' call for you to remain in the world will be challenging. There will be times when the world hates you. It hated him as well. Even so, the Father needed to send his Son. He couldn't do the work he wanted to do in this world unless Jesus entered a stable in Bethlehem. Likewise, you cannot do the work Jesus calls you to do unless you are in the world.

As you do Jesus' work in the world, he is praying that you will be kept from the evil one. Satan hates you just as he hated Jesus. He wants to kill, steal, and destroy. Learn about his wiles and resist them. Stand firmly against him. When you do, he will flee.

Don't allow the world to conform you to its pernicious priorities. You are a citizen of Christ's kingdom. You are dead to the gods of this world. Live by the Lord's standards. Your old life has passed away. A new one has come. Your heart's desire should be to glorify Jesus.

You are in the world, but not of the world.

As salt, you make people thirsty to know the Lord. As light, you enable people to walk in truth toward him.

Today, live for Jesus in the world.

Walk closely with him and carefully for him. Work willingly and with enthusiasm at whatever you do. The Lord is your boss, not people. You are serving him. Show love to everyone you meet.

Ask people about their needs. Write them down and pray for them. If possible, let them know you're praying for them. If answers come, see them marvel on God's gracious responses.

Be a funnel of God's grace and mercy to all with whom you come in contact. Your mission field is wherever you are, caring for the people around you at that moment. Wherever you may be affords you a grand opportunity to serve the Lord.

Be generous in all you give. You are like a farmer sowing seeds into the world. If you sow sparingly, you will reap sparingly. But if you sow abundantly, you will reap abundantly. You will experience a generous crop.

Be in the world. Be faithful as you work in the world. Be generous in all you give.

Do this, and one day you will hear Jesus say, "Well done, good and faithful servant."

✳ ✳

A Purpose for God's Word

Today's Reading: John 17:17-19

HEARING GOD'S VOICE FOR TODAY:
"Sanctify them in the truth; your word is truth."

✳ ✳ ✳

One of Jesus' ongoing prayers to the Father is that you will be sanctified. This is a lifelong process. Over time, you are being conformed to Jesus' image. He is working in you daily to make you holy in the same way that his Father in heaven is holy.

This process begins when you are born of the Holy Spirit. Notice he is "holy." When he invades your heart and takes up residence, the process of being separated from the world and its evil influences begins. You start to grow in godliness, morality, and holiness.

As this takes place, you are being conformed to Jesus' image. Your attitudes and actions start to look like his. You are more like him than you were yesterday, but probably not as much as you will be tomorrow. It is a daily, grueling, grinding, and lifelong process. Only in heaven will you be fully sanctified.

The main way sanctification occurs in you is by learning truth. There is objective, moral truth in this world. The world teaches differently—that all truth is relative. It says that truth is only as you perceive it—even if it's contrary to another person's view of truth.

That view is a postmodern lie. It reflects the darkness of the world. It allows everyone to do what is right in his own eyes. It's a very dangerous place for any individual and culture to be.

Truth is found in the Word of God. It is his eternal, inerrant truth. He wrote it. He breathed it. It's never conformed to the world's standards. Everything in this world must be measured, tested by, and compared to God's Word, which is ultimate truth.

Your personal holiness will grow when you study, ingest, and obey God's Word. It reveals the world's lies. And it shows you the Lord's true ways—the ways in which you should walk.

You should meditate on God's Word day and night, as opportunities come your way. As you do so, you will be sure to obey everything written in it. Only then will you prosper and succeed in all you do.[12]

As you follow the truths in his Word, sanctification occurs. His Word teaches, corrects, reproves, and trains you toward holiness and right living. Its truths make you live, look, and act more and more like Jesus every day. It rids you of all the filth and evil in you. It sets you free to be who God desires you to be. And God's Word remains forever.

The Lord's will for you is not to make you happy, but holy.

It's not to make you comfortable, but to conform you to Jesus' image.

That happens as you study and obey his Word. There's no shortcut. But blessed are all who hear God's Word and put it into practice.

God's Word is true.

Pursue Unity

Today's Reading: John 17:20-26

HEARING GOD'S VOICE FOR TODAY:

"I do not ask for these only, but also for those who will believe in me through their word, that they may all be one, just as you, Father, are in me, and I in you, that they also may be in us, so that the world may believe that you have sent me. The glory that you have given me I have given to them, that they may be one even as we are one."

✳ ✳ ✳

When Jesus came to the Father in prayer in John 17, he not only prayed for the disciples who were with him, but also for all who will ever believe in him. That includes you right now—if you believe in him.

Jesus' prayer for you has one specific concern: He wants all his followers to be unified. He wants them to be one in the same way that he and his Father are one. He is perfectly in the Father, and the Father in him.

When you receive Christ as Savior, he enters you. And if the Father and the Son are perfectly one, that means they both indwell you. That's an example of the unity they desire among all believers. When the world sees this unity being lived out, it will believe that the Father sent the Son to forgive their sins.

The Father and the Son desire all believers to remain unified. United we stand against the enemy, divided we fall. A kingdom divided internally cannot stand. We need one another to advance the Lord's kingdom.

A sports team cannot succeed if divided. Nor can a business organization. Nor can a marriage. There must be unity. Conversely, individual fingers can cause little harm—giving only a painless poke. But balled together, the fingers can become a fist, and a powerful force.

The devil's name means "the divider." He wants to divide friendships, marriages, and churches. He knows the power of unity. He knows defeat is difficult when believers stand together. That's why he desires division and uses every available tool in his hellish arsenal to separate believers.

That's why Jesus instructs you to pursue unity with all your energy.

If you've hurt one of his followers, before you attend another worship service, drop everything and go reconcile yourself with that person.[13] If you don't, then your worship will make a mockery of God's forgiveness freely given to you. He wants unity.

If someone has hurt you, pray for him to be blessed by the Lord. It's impossible to feel bitterness while you are praying for someone to receive God's blessings. Forgive. Be freed from bitterness. If possible, make every effort to be at peace with others. Jesus wants unity.

If your marriage is being threatened by divorce, fight hard to stay married. Your children will be hurt the most if you break apart. For the rest of their lives, they will carry around the scars of mom and dad separating. Plus, it's a terrible witness for Christ before a watching world. He wants unity.

Make every effort to guard your unity—in your friendships, marriages, and the church.

There's great power in unity, as the Father and the Son well know.

✳ ✳

The Cup of God's Wrath

Today's Reading: John 18:1-11

HEARING GOD'S VOICE FOR TODAY:
"Then Simon Peter, having a sword, drew it and struck the high priest's servant and cut off his right ear. (The servant's name was Malchus.) So Jesus said to Peter, 'Put your sword into its sheath; shall I not drink the cup that the Father has given to me?'"

✳ ✳ ✳

Simon Peter was incensed that Jesus was being arrested. Earlier, Peter had promised that he would die for the Lord. True to his word, he took action to defend Jesus.

Peter removed a short sword that was hidden under his garment. This kind of sword was used for stabbing, not slicing. A quick jab rightly aimed at a vital organ would cause immediate death.

Peter drew his sword and attacked Malchus, the high priest's servant. He aimed for his head, but instead, cut off the servant's ear. Jesus immediately healed Malchus's ear. He wanted to teach his followers that if they lived by the sword, they would die by the sword.

Jesus also used this moment to teach the disciples another important truth about his mission on earth. He wanted them to know what it meant for him to drink the cup the Father had given to him.

The "cup" was a metaphor for God's judgment. Throughout the Old Testament, it was always used as a symbol of the Father's coming wrath. The Father gave it to the Son to drink from for the forgiveness of your sins.

Jesus' greatest agony on earth was not the physical pain of the crucifixion. Though excruciating, it could not begin to compare with the spiritual agony he faced while he was on the cross. There, he took the Father's wrath upon himself. He bore the sins of all humankind when he drank from this cup. He was separated from his Father in heaven when he absorbed all our sins upon his body.

This was why, when Jesus prayed earlier in the garden of Gethsemane, he asked the Father if there was a way other than the cross. After all, his greatest joy was being one in a perfect relationship with the Father. But when Jesus became a substitute for our sins, their unity was torn apart. The Father could not have fellowship with Jesus because he had taken upon himself all the sins of the world. The Father forsook his Son.

The cross was always the Father's will for the Son. His heart of love for you demanded that Jesus drink of the cup of his wrath so you wouldn't have to. Jesus gladly submitted to the Father's will because he knew it would allow you the forgiveness of your sins and a right relationship with them forever.

Do you believe this? Do you believe that the Father's anger was poured out on Jesus instead of you? Do you believe the Father is ready to forgive you if you just ask him to?

It is true. Through Jesus, your sins are forever forgiven—as far as the east is from the west. Regarding your sins, the Father is an eternal amnesiac. They are remembered no more, blotted out for Christ's sake. Though like scarlet, he has made them white as snow.

And you can now know the joy of his salvation and a clean heart and a renewed spirit.

Be Strong and Courageous

Today's Reading: John 18:12-18

HEARING GOD'S VOICE FOR TODAY:
*"Simon Peter followed Jesus, and so did another disciple.
Since that disciple was known to the high priest, he entered
with Jesus into the court of the high priest, but Peter stood
outside at the door. So the other disciple, who was known
to the high priest, went out and spoke to the servant girl
who kept watch at the door, and brought Peter in."*

✳ ✳ ✳

All the other disciples had fled except two—Peter, and another one who was unnamed. He was John, the author of this Gospel. Once again he was deferential about revealing his identity, and because of this, we know who he was.

Peter and John followed Jesus to "the court of the high priest," an enclosed space with no roof, meaning one could look up and see the sky. Peter stayed outside the gate, while John entered. He was known to the high priest and was able to enter.

There was a servant girl guarding the courtyard. John went to her and vouched for Peter, and she allowed him to enter.

Peter and John's courage should be noted. All the other disciples had fled. By contrast, John and Peter desired to be faithful to the Lord. They had followed the entourage that had arrested him because they feared something awful might happen to him.

In the face of enormous adversity, they chose to follow Jesus. They were very courageous.

What is courage? It is not being ignorant about the future and yet still moving forward. Rather, true courage is clearly knowing what awaits you but still choosing to move ahead. It's unflinchingly staring the enemy in the face while not knowing what the eventual outcome may be.

Jesus is always looking for courageous followers—disciples who might not know what's awaiting them but are still willing to march into hell for a heavenly cause. He needs people who will be unabashed witnesses for him—both in word and deed. He needs fearless helpers who will act to advance the Father's kingdom on earth.

Yes, Peter would go on to deny the Lord. But at least he was in the courtyard. At least he hadn't run away as the others had. John and Peter resisted cowardice. They went inside the courtyard. They knew doing this was dangerous, but still they followed their Master.

Emulate Peter and John. Be strong and courageous for Jesus. Do not panic or be afraid of those who may criticize or threaten you. What can they do to you? Jesus will guard you from all sides. He won't fail or abandon you. He will fight for you and give you victory.

Jesus will arm you with his strength. He will go ahead of you in the battle. The battle belongs to him. In fact, he has already won the battle!

Jesus knows you by name. You are his. Knowing these truths should give you enormous confidence. You can be very bold.

He will make your way perfect. He is your sun and your shield. He is your shelter and refuge. He is your strong tower. He watches over every area of your life. He will protect you from danger.

Why should you tremble?

Trust him with all your heart.

God's Plans Are Perfect

Today's Reading: John 18:19-24

HEARING GOD'S VOICE FOR TODAY:
"When he had said these things, one of the officers standing by struck Jesus with his hand, saying, 'Is that how you answer the high priest?' Jesus answered him, 'If what I said is wrong, bear witness about the wrong; but if what I said is right, why do you strike me?' Annas then sent him bound to Caiaphas."

✳ ✳ ✳

Annas was the former high priest—back when Jesus had cleansed the Temple three years earlier. That had embarrassed Annas, so he despised Jesus. He had wanted to exact some revenge, though he didn't have any authority to do so at that time.

Annas asked Jesus about his teaching. Jesus told him to talk with those who had listened to him in the synagogues and Temple. That led one of the nearby guards to strike Jesus. He thought Jesus was being insolent and disrespectful.

The guard's blow was another way Jesus took your punishment for sin upon himself. He endured great injustice because of his great love for you.

But there's another truth here that the Lord wants you to ponder.

There are times when you should not try to defend yourself. Some hours later, when Jesus was before Herod, he refused to respond to him and defend himself. He knew it was useless for him to say anything to Herod.

But with Annas, Jesus did the opposite. There are times when it's necessary to defend yourself—especially when the accusations aren't truthful. The guard thought Jesus to be insolent. But Jesus knew that he'd spoken nothing but the truth. As God's law says in Exodus 22:28: "You shall not revile God, nor curse a ruler of your people." Jesus had not cursed Annas, nor had he reviled God. He was perfectly within his rights to defend himself.

Truthful self-defense is not sinful. If someone is maliciously spreading lies about you, it is perfectly acceptable for you to defend yourself. You can set the record straight. If you don't, who will?

People will revile you because you love Jesus. Lies will be spread about you. The father of lies will work behind the scenes to slander your name. But don't despair. Though they can kill the body, they can't touch your soul. Speak the truth in love. Stand courageously for the Lord. He will give you the words to speak when you need them.

He will do that because his love for you is so great.

Annas then sent Jesus to Caiaphas, who despised him as well. The plot to kill Jesus was inching forward. The plan to make salvation available to the world was advancing as well.

None of the Father's plans can be thwarted. This is true for everything in the world. All human history is God's story.

It's true in your personal life as well. He knew you while you were being formed in your mother's womb. He knew you by name before the world was ever created.

God's purpose for your life is perfect.

No weapon formed against you will prosper.

✳ ✳

You Can Always Begin Again

Today's Reading: John 18:25-27

HEARING GOD'S VOICE FOR TODAY:
"Peter again denied it, and at once the rooster crowed."

✳ ✳ ✳

Back when Jesus had washed Peter's feet, he predicted that Peter would deny him three times before the rooster finished crowing. It would be a moment of intense shame for Peter.

That prediction came true. As Peter stood in the high priest's courtyard, he denied knowing the Lord—three times. The final denial was spoken to one of Malchus's relatives. (Malchus was the one whose ear Peter had cut off in the garden of Gethsemane.) Then the rooster crowed.

There were times when Peter was impetuously courageous. For example, when Jesus called Peter to become a follower, he immediately dropped his nets and did so. Later, during a storm, he was the only disciple to jump out of the boat and walk on water toward Jesus. And the night before the Lord went to the cross, Peter boastfully proclaimed he'd be willing to die for him.

But Peter also had times of embarrassing cowardice. When he faced his own crucible in the courtyard, he denied he knew Jesus. In the Lord's hour of greatest need, Peter failed him.

In fact, Peter did exactly what Judas had done. He betrayed Jesus. But Peter returned to Jesus. He experienced Jesus' gracious forgiveness. He repented and and was restored to fellowship and friendship with Jesus.

Godly sorrow always leads to repentance. That was not the case for Judas. He felt sorrow, but was too proud to ask for forgiveness. Jesus would have immediately given it to him. Even at the last supper, the Lord purposely seated Judas to his left—the position of honor. Up till the last moment, Jesus yearned for him to repent. But Judas stubbornly refused.

The Savior will not force repentance on anyone. Not even the city of Jerusalem, which he had wanted to gather under his wings as a mother hen does her brood. But she refused.

Godly sorrow leads to repentance. That is the deep feeling of regret that wants to change the behavior that initially broke the Father's heart. It changes life's trajectory and moves in a direction away from sin. It receives grace that restores a life broken by sin. It rescues those with a crushed spirit.

Jesus will never reject a contrite and repentant heart. He entered this world to save sinners. He is gracious and merciful. If you return to him, you will live. He will never turn his face from you if you return to him.

Jesus loves to give second chances. Just look at Peter.

Jesus restored Peter with his grace and made him a rock in his kingdom.

Let him do so with you as well.

❋ ❋

All Authority Comes from Jesus

Today's Reading: John 19:1-11

Hearing God's Voice for Today:

"So Pilate said to him, 'You will not speak to me? Do you not know that I have authority to release you and authority to crucify you?' Jesus answered him, 'You would have no authority over me at all unless it had been given you from above. Therefore, he who delivered me over to you has the greater sin.'"

❋ ❋ ❋

Pilate was caught in a vise. The Jewish leaders wanted Jesus dead. But Pilate found no guilt in him. And his wife had an intuition in a dream that led her to warn him not to have anything to do with Jesus.[14]

The Roman soldiers shoved a crown of thorns on Jesus' forehead, causing a swollen, bloodied brow. They hung a purple robe on his shoulders to mock his claim to be a king.

But the crowd's blind rage still demanded his death.

Pilate asked Jesus where he came from. The Lord didn't answer. Pilate became increasingly irritated and asked Jesus if he fully understood that he had all authority to set him free or kill him.

Jesus responded. He knew that there is a time to be silent and there is a time to speak. Now was a time to speak in his defense—to address Pilate's misstatement.

Jesus told Pilate that he had no authority unless it had been given to him from above, from the heavenly Father. He rules over all earthly authorities, whether they realize it or not. He alone exalts and lowers people. No human has power unless the Father gives it to him.

Every earthly leader will one day face the heavenly Father. They will be held responsible for how they've treated his children. Jesus also reminded Pilate that Caiaphas, the one who had handed him over, had committed the greater sin. He was the master overseer guiding this scenario from behind the scenes. Pilate was a mere puppet. Caiaphas would be held to a stricter wrath from the Father because he clearly knew what he was doing.

All sin is wrong before the Father. But there are greater and lesser sins in the Father's moral law.[15] Some sins inflict greater pain on people than other sins. The greater the sin, the greater the judgment will be from the heavenly Father. That was true for Caiaphas. It is true for all people in authority.

If you oversee others, you need to recognize this truth: If you have any authority on earth and are influencing others, either in your job, or at home with kids, or in an organization, realize that all authority has been given to you from above. Therefore, use your authority wisely. Use it to influence people toward Jesus. Use it to care for others, not gain personal benefits. Use it to help people, not hurt them.

The best leaders serve people for those people's glory. They don't use people for their own glory. They are true servant leaders. They are not proud or arrogant. They operate in humility and grace. They see the oversight of others as a gift from God. They realize that one day they will be accountable to God for how they've treated those under their authority. They take this leadership responsibility very seriously.

After all, Jesus said that all authority in heaven and on earth has been given to him.[16] Human ability to oversee others is a gift from him.

All earthly leaders need to be reminded they are under Jesus' leadership.

Human leadership needs to reflect his servant leadership.

No Greater Love

Today's Reading: John 19:12-16

HEARING GOD'S VOICE FOR TODAY:
*"Now it was the day of the preparation of the Passover. It
was about the sixth hour. He said to the Jews, 'Behold
your King!' They cried out, 'Away with him, away with
him, crucify him!' Pilate said to them, 'Shall I crucify your
King?' The chief priests answered, 'We have no king but
Caesar.' So he delivered him over to them to be crucified."*

✳ ✳ ✳

It was the day of the preparation for the Passover. The Passover lambs were being prepared in the Temple area to be slaughtered for the sins of the people. And Jesus was being prepared as well, as the Lamb of God who would take away the sins of the world.

Pilate brought Jesus into the courtyard— beaten and bedraggled. He said, "Behold, your King!" The mob yelled back, "Away with him, crucify him!" Pilate responded, "Shall I crucify your King?" They retorted, "We have no king but Caesar."

Astonishingly, the crowd acknowledged Caesar, not God, as their king. They subverted their own national heritage. They committed blasphemy—the very crime they accused Jesus of committing! God had repeatedly told his people only he could be their King.[17] Yet the people denied their own messianic expectations of a king who would come and free them from Roman oppression.

Seeing this intensely obdurate opposition, Pilate had no other option. To maintain his power and prevent a rebellion, he was forced to give Jesus over to be crucified.

With the death sentence pronounced, Jesus received 39 lashes. This act was nicknamed "intermediate death." A whip was matted with metal, glass, and bone. Each lash bit deeply into the Savior's flesh, ripping apart skin, muscle, and sinew. The purpose was to weaken the body so death would not linger on the cross.

Jesus went through all this agony for you. Those lashes should have been yours. Your sin caused great alienation between you and the heavenly Father. But Jesus took the punishment for your sin upon himself so you wouldn't have to receive it.

That's how much he loves you.

Could there be a greater love in the universe than that of Jesus laying down his life for you? A friend would die for a friend, but who would suffer and die for an enemy? Jesus suffered excruciating agony so you wouldn't have to. He gave his life for you. He died in your place.

Jesus knew no sin, yet he became sin so that you might become the righteousness of God.[18] The proof of this love is that while you were still wallowing in your sin, he died for you. He didn't wait for you to try to become perfect before he went to the cross to die for your sins.

What more could he give you?

Contemplate and grasp today the depth, breadth, width, and height of his love for you. Believe it's true. It's lavish and without limit. Claim it for yourself. Cling to it no matter what you're facing.

And you'll discover he is able to do in and through you more than you could ever think or imagine.

Honor Your Parents

Today's Reading: John 19:17-27

HEARING GOD'S VOICE FOR TODAY:
*"Standing by the cross of Jesus were his mother and his mother's
sister, Mary, the wife of Clopas, and Mary Magdalene.
When Jesus saw his mother and the disciple whom he loved
standing nearby, he said to his mother, 'Woman, behold your
son!' Then he said to the disciple, 'Behold your mother!' And
from that hour the disciple took her to his own home."*

✳ ✳ ✳

Pilate ordered Jesus to be crucified. He was nailed to the cross, and people waited for him to die.

At the foot of the cross were Jesus' closest friends and relatives. There was his mother, Mary. She had carried him in her womb. Now she awaited him placed in a tomb.

Mary's sister, Salome, was there as well. She was the mother of James and John, two of the disciples. Mary Magdalene was present. She had experienced a dramatic life change when Jesus had freed her from past bondages. She'd become a new creation because of his grace.

And there was John. All the other disciples had fled in fear. They were convinced they too would be arrested and crucified. But John stayed true to the end. How great was his love and courage! He was truly the disciple whom Jesus loved.

Even in his last moments on earth, Jesus remained committed to perfectly obeying the Father's moral law. The Ten Commandments were given by the heavenly Father to express his heart of perfect righteousness. Therefore, as death neared, Jesus desired to obey the command to honor his parents.[19] He wanted to make provision for his mother after he died. She was a widow. She had no income or anyone to take care of her.

So Jesus turned to Mary and said, "Woman." It was a term of endearment. He loved her deeply. She was a woman of extraordinary faith and obedience.

Jesus said to his mother, "Behold your son." He wanted her to know that John would now be responsible for caring for her for the rest of her life. Jesus then pointed her to his dear friend John and told her he was now her son. From that moment onward, John took Mary into his home. He made sure her every earthly need was addressed until she died and went home to be with the Lord.

The lesson here is clear: Do the same for your parents. To honor your parents is one of the Ten Commandments. It's also the only one that has a promise connected to it: You will live long in the land.

Yes, the Lord understands your situation if you had bad parents. If they abused you, you don't have to let them continually abuse you. But you are still commanded to honor them. That means you pray for them. You forgive them for any wrong they've done to you. Perhaps because of your love for Jesus that is expressed in the ways you minister to your parents as they age, they will repent and seek forgiveness from God.

And remember this truth: You will age as well. Your children are watching you as you care for your parents. Your example will determine how they care for you.

As you honor your parents, the Lord will honor you. It's a moral requirement from him. Always honor your parents.

Jesus did so with his mother. Do so with your parents.

✳ ✳

It Is Finished

Today's Reading: John 19:28-30

HEARING GOD'S VOICE FOR TODAY:
"After this, Jesus, knowing that all was now finished,
said (to fulfill the Scripture), 'I thirst'...When Jesus
had received the sour wine, he said, 'It is finished,'
and he bowed his head and gave up his spirit."

✳ ✳ ✳

Jesus knew death was near. He knew his work on earth was almost complete.

Before he died, he said, "I thirst." There was a specific reason. He was fulfilling a specific prophecy. Psalm 22 is a messianic psalm. It looks forward to the Savior and addresses the righteous one of God suffering in thirst (verse 15).

Every word of God's Word is true. The Holy Spirit authored it. It was not written by fiat. Every word in it was written for a reason.

The Savior's thirst on the cross shows his humanity. He was totally divine and human at the same time. Because of his humanity, there is no temptation that you face that he is not aware of. When you become weary, remember that he became weary. When you feel alone, know that he felt the same way. He desired human relationships, as you do. He faced death, as you do. He became thirsty, as you do.

That means there's nothing you experience in this life that he doesn't understand. As your eternal friend, you can lean on him with all your burdens. He understands them all. He empathizes with your every hurt. He will help you carry them.

Then, after Jesus drank the sour wine, he said, "It is finished," and he died.

What is the "it" that Jesus finished? "It" is the finished work of your salvation. He had completed the work on earth for which he'd been sent. Where Adam had failed to obey God's moral law, Jesus was successful. He had finished living the perfect, sinless, and righteous life no human could ever live. He had met every single aspect of the righteous requirements of God's law.

Jesus had to be perfect God and perfect man for forgiveness to occur. He had to be perfect man and meet the law's requirements to substitute his life for yours. He had to be perfect God to pay the price for your sin. God is the offended party with your sin. Only he can grant forgiveness.

Jesus bore the penalty for your sin. Your debt to the heavenly Father was paid in full. Jesus' obedience to what the Father had asked him to do was now complete.

Jesus "gave up" his life. His spirit was released from his body. In three days, it would be covered in a new, glorious, and perfect resurrection body.

On the cross, the Savior finished the work of righteousness you could not accomplish. He now offers you the forgiveness of your sins through his completed work on the cross. It's a gift offered to you, the gift of eternal life—all by grace through faith.

Have you received this free gift today? Yes, it's easy for you to obtain. But it cost the heavenly Father everything to make it easy for you to receive—even the death of his only Son. But he desired to make salvation easy for you because of his great love for you.

He loves each of us like there is only one of us.

If you have received this free gift, your sins are forgiven. You need never fear death. You have eternal security in the Lord.

It's guaranteed by Jesus' finished work.

Jesus Was Dead

Today's Reading: John 19:31-37

HEARING GOD'S VOICE FOR TODAY:
*"When they came to Jesus and saw that he was already dead, they
did not break his legs. But one of the soldiers pierced his side
with a spear, and at once there came out blood and water."*

✳ ✳ ✳

Pilate had agreed to take down the bodies of the crucified prisoners before nightfall. He instructed the guards to go and break their
legs. This would cause death by asphyxiation. The broken legs would
prevent the prisoners from pushing up on the cross with their legs so
they could continue to breathe.

The two criminals on either side of Jesus had their legs broken
because they were still alive. They died soon thereafter.

But when the guards came to Jesus, they saw that he was already
dead, so they did not break his legs. However, to be completely sure,
they took a long spear with an iron point and pierced it into his side.
Blood and water poured forth. Through the ages, medical experts have
looked upon this fact as evidence that Jesus was dead. Blood and water
mingled together means a person is dead.

Why is this important? For centuries, preposterous theories have
been proposed to dismiss the Lord's resurrection. One of them is called
the "swoon theory." It suggests Jesus wasn't really dead on the cross.
He was taken down alive and placed in a dark, dank, and damp tomb.
There, his body was refreshed. He regained his strength and went to
his disciples and convinced them he had risen. They then continued
to carry out Jesus' ministry of hope and love to others.

Why is this theory preposterous? Think about all Jesus had experienced during his final hours. He'd gotten no sleep the night before. He received severe beatings. The 39 lashes on his back had been nicknamed "intermediate death" by the Romans because of the severity of this punishment. Some prisoners didn't survive it. He hung six hours on the cross—each moment taking him closer to asphyxiation. There was a spear stuck into his side.

Jesus was then taken down from the cross and placed in a tomb. After several hours, in the middle of the night, he was supposedly resuscitated. He then moved a huge stone weighing approximately one ton. He was then able to elude crack Roman guards and find his disciples, who were hiding in fear. He showed them his broken, bruised, and beaten body as a resurrection hope they needed to give the world.

It doesn't make sense. How could Jesus' bloodied and beaten body give them hope for their new and perfect resurrection body?

It also means they made up the story of Jesus being dead and then God raising him to new life. Why is this important? It suggests the disciples suffered persecution and martyrdom for what they knew was a lie. But people don't willingly die for what they know is a lie. They may die for what they think is true about God but isn't really true. But no one suffers and dies for what they know is a lie. It's against human nature. People are too self-protective. That's not how they operate.

Jesus was dead. The Roman guards, who were experienced at determining when people died, knew he was dead. It's why they didn't break his legs. It's why he was placed in a tomb.

People make up fanciful theories about Jesus for one reason: They don't want to yield their lives to him. They don't want to place moral reins on their life's lusts and passions. They want to be lord of their own lives.

Jesus had to be dead for the resurrection to be valid. He was crucified, died, and was buried. The "swoon theory" is frivolous. He was dead. The mixture of blood and water proves it. The early church placed this fact in their creedal statements (1 Corinthians 15:3-4). It's an essential bulwark of the Christian faith. It must be believed for the resurrection to make sense.

Jesus' death and resurrection has great significance for you. When you die, if you believe in him, you too will be raised to new life.

That means you can shout with confidence these words: "Hallelujah, Christ is risen!"

And you can also cry out, "Hallelujah, I am risen as well!"

The Body Is in the Tomb

Today's Reading: John 19:38-42

HEARING GOD'S VOICE FOR TODAY:
*"Now in the place where he was crucified there was a garden,
and in the garden a new tomb in which no one had been
laid. So because of the Jewish day of Preparation, since
the tomb was close at hand, they laid Jesus there."*

✳ ✳ ✳

When Jesus was taken down from the cross, Joseph of Arimathea, a wealthy member of the Sanhedrin, gave over use of his tomb in devotion to the Lord. It was new; no one had ever been laid in it. Nicodemus, another member of the Sanhedrin, provided burial spices with which to anoint Jesus' body.

The Lord's body then was wrapped in linen cloths and burial spices. These linen cloths are sometimes called *swaddling cloths*. Ironically, when Jesus departed the world, he was dressed the same way as when he entered it.

The Jewish day of preparation was at hand. Jesus was laid in the tomb right before the Sabbath was to begin and all work must cease— including carrying linen wrappings, spices, and a dead corpse. Everything had been completed quickly for his burial.

Then a large stone was rolled in front of the tomb. It was sealed to assure no one could enter. After all, on several occasions, Jesus had prophesied that he would be crucified and raised from the dead. If this seal was broken and the body stolen, the guards would have to pay the price of the condemned prisoner. In this case, the guards overseeing Jesus' body would face crucifixion themselves if his body was taken.

Everyone left the tomb except the Roman guards. They were highly motivated to make sure Jesus' body remained there. Pilate and the Jewish leaders did not want to take a chance on Jesus rising from the dead, or his disciples stealing the body. They wanted the certainty of his dead body in the tomb to squelch any rumors about a resurrection.

Is it important for people to know the actual location of Jesus' actual burial site? Most likely, no. Through the centuries, people have debated where his body was actually laid. In Jerusalem, there are three potential burial sites that historians point to and people visit.

No one knows with certainty the true burial site. That is probably God's preference. He wouldn't want people worshiping a shrine where they think Jesus was buried. People love to worship places and build monuments that end up becoming a substitute for an authentic faith.

God may have purposely hidden the burial place, just as he hid Moses's burial place. He understands human nature. He knows how people are prone to worship creation instead of the Creator. He wants them to worship him alone.

At the same time, consider this: All three potential burial sites have one thing in common: Each one is empty. Jesus is not in any of them.

And rest assured of this: If any of Jesus' enemies could have produced a body to show that he had never risen, they would have. Show his corpse, and his movement is finished. But no one could. He has risen from the dead. He is alive!

The grave could not hold him. Death could not contain him. His victory over sin and death is complete.

And if you believe in him, your victory is certain as well.

Who Moved the Stone?

Today's Reading: John 20:1-5

HEARING GOD'S VOICE FOR TODAY:
"Now on the first day of the week Mary Magdalene came to the tomb early, while it was still dark, and saw that the stone had been taken away from the tomb."

✳ ✳ ✳

Mary Magdalene went to Jesus' tomb early on Sunday morning. It was the first day of the week. Soon thereafter, Jesus' followers started worshiping him on this day. It was to honor the day of his resurrection from the dead.

That Christ is worshiped on Sunday is another proof he was raised from the dead. Think about it. For more than a millennium, Jews had faithfully worshiped God on Saturday. Yet in a brief period of time, Christians changed this sacred worship day. Plus, they worshiped *Jesus* on this day. There is one major reason: They had seen him alive. It was a way to honor the importance of the resurrection.

The resurrection proves not only that Jesus is God, but that he is also worthy of worship.

The other Gospel accounts share that Mary Magdalene was not alone at the tomb. There were other women with her. You always want to make sure you read these accounts alongside one another so you will have the most complete picture of what happened. Good detectives always talk to multiple witnesses so they can put together the full story of what happened. Their gathering of independent accounts can help prove there was no corroboration.

When the women arrived, they saw that the large stone that had been placed in front of the tomb had been rolled away. And they couldn't find Jesus' body.

Mary Magdalene pondered a very significant question: Who moved the stone? It's a question of great importance. Your answer determines your eternal destination.

Not knowing what had happened, Mary Magdalene concluded the Roman authorities had moved the stone. That's one option. But why would they? They were clearly instructed by Pilate to guard the tomb and make sure no one moved the stone and stole Jesus' body. Plus, if the body had been stolen, they would have to suffer the penalty of the person whose body was gone. That means they would have been crucified themselves. They were highly motivated to keep Jesus' body in the tomb.

Others since have suggested the Jewish authorities had moved the stone and stolen the body. But the question asked about the Roman authorities must similarly be asked here: Why would they? They wanted all resurrection rumors squelched. They had nothing to gain by stealing Jesus' body.

Still others say the disciples rolled away the stone and stole Jesus' body. But was this possible? How could a ragtag group of forlorn, discouraged men elude crack Roman guards, move the huge stone, and steal the body? It makes no rational sense. Also, they were hiding for their lives. They thought persecution and death would come to them as it had for their Master. Why would they make themselves readily available to potential arrest and crucifixion?

There is really only one remaining option for who moved the stone: God did. And he moved the stone not to let Jesus out, but to let you in. He wanted everyone, for all time, to see that the tomb was empty.

Jesus was no longer there. The tomb was empty. He is alive!

And now you know this good news: Because of Jesus' resurrection, when you place your faith in him, your sins are forever forgiven.

Your heart can rest in this hope—today and every day you will ever face.

✳ ✳

Jesus' Resurrection Power Lives in You

Today's Reading: John 20:6-10

HEARING GOD'S VOICE FOR TODAY:
"He saw the linen cloths lying there, and the face cloth, which had been on Jesus' head, not lying with the linen cloths but folded up in a place by itself. Then the other disciple, who had reached the tomb first, also went in, and he saw and believed; for as yet they did not understand the Scripture, that he must rise from the dead."

✳ ✳ ✳

When Mary Magdalene told Peter and John that the stone had been rolled away, they ran to the tomb. John arrived first and glanced inside. Peter then arrived. In deference to age and prominence, John let Peter enter first.

A couple things caught their attention in the tomb. They noticed the linen cloths without a body inside. Perhaps it seemed like Jesus' body had been supernaturally removed, thus causing the linen cloths to collapse in an ordered heap.

They also noticed the facial napkin, used to keep a deceased person's jaw shut. It was neatly folded in a place by itself. When Jesus left the tomb, he practiced good manners! He was concerned about the smallest, most appropriate details of life—including yours.

These observations led them to conclude and believe that the Lord was alive.

The heavenly Father was also careful to make sure that every detail of the Jewish law was covered with regard to testimonies given about evidence. There needed to be two male witnesses to corroborate a story.[20] Peter and John's witness about Jesus' resurrection fulfilled this aspect of God's law.

It's also quite remarkable that the first person to whom Jesus entrusted his resurrection message was a woman. Yes, Peter and John's witness confirmed her story so the requirements of the Jewish law would be met. But Jesus gave the first responsibility to tell this good news to a woman. The Lord was setting the stage for a church that would see male and female as equal participants in his kingdom.

Notice that until this moment, Peter and John did not believe Jesus had risen. This proves they didn't make up a fanciful story to give support to his predictions of a resurrection. It was only *after* they had been presented with the facts that they believed.

Do you believe that Jesus was raised from the dead? The resurrection proves his divinity. As someone jokingly said, "You can't keep a good God down." If Jesus is God in human flesh, he cannot remain dead, lying in a tomb. He must come back to life.

Examine the evidence. Look at all the prophecies and stories in the Old Testament that point to him. When Jesus showed this evidence to two of his disciples on the road from Jerusalem to Emmaus, it helped them believe.[21] They observed the prophecy that he would crush the head of the serpent.[22] They saw the specifics of how he had suffered on the cross.[23] They concluded he was the suffering servant who was to come and save Israel.[24] After examining these texts and many others, they believed that he indeed had been raised from the dead.

Believe in him as well.

When you do, the same power that raised Jesus from the dead will live in you. He will be your strength and shield, your light and salvation. He will be your strong tower. You will be able to run to him and be safe.[25]

And he will care for every detail of your life.

The God of Angelic Armies

Today's Reading: John 20:11-14

HEARING GOD'S VOICE FOR TODAY:
"As she wept she stooped to look into the tomb. And she saw two angels in white, sitting where the body of Jesus had lain, one at the head and one at the feet."

* * *

Peter and John saw and believed. They ran from the tomb to tell the other disciples what they had seen. They were overcome with joy.

But Mary Magdalene remained behind, outside the tomb. She had not yet concluded that Jesus had been raised from the dead.

She looked into the tomb and saw two angels sitting on the stone slab where Jesus had once been laid. One was sitting where his head had been placed, the other where his feet once were. They were dressed in white, expressing their perfect, sinless, and brilliant purity.

The Father in heaven is often called "the Lord of hosts." This means that he is the Lord of all the angelic armies. There are millions upon millions of these magnificent creatures who worship God continually. And they also serve as messengers sent forth from heaven to help God's elect who will inherit salvation.

The Father sent two of these mighty messengers to the empty tomb to tell Mary Magdalene the good news that Jesus was alive. Amidst her grief, they gave her hope. Her mourning soon turned to joy.

The heavenly Father oversees all these angels. He wants his children to understand and use this underutilized spiritual power. They are available to you as they were to Mary Magdalene and all the saints through the ages.

If you are in distress today, ask your heavenly Father to send you his angels to help you. They do his bidding and obey his word. The Father commands them to carefully guard you in all your ways. They can go before you. They can be your rear guard. They can oversee your right and left flanks. They desire to minister to you.

And they are always on your side, fighting for you against all your enemies.

The Father who oversees the entire world oversees his angelic armies. Ask for them. They are available to you. If there's a delay, persevere in prayer, believing they are coming to you. Trust that if you could see in the invisible, spiritual, and eternal world, there would be more angels than demons. They far outnumber the enemy forces that are against you—two of God's angels for every demon (Revelation 12:4). That reality should cause you never to fear demonic hordes.

Nothing formed against you will stand.[26] The Father holds the entire world—and you—in his hands. He is faithful to all the promises he has made to you.

The Lord of hosts, the King over all the angelic armies, is ready to send them to you.

Are you ready to ask for them?

✳ ✳

God Is Your Loving Daddy

Today's Reading: John 20:15-18

Hearing God's Voice for Today:
*"Jesus said to her, 'Do not cling to me, for I have not yet ascended
to my Father and your Father, to my God and your God.'
Mary Magdalene went and announced to the disciples, 'I have
seen the Lord'—and that he had said these things to her."*

✳ ✳ ✳

Mary Magdalene had gone to Jesus' tomb and found his body missing. When he asked her, "Why are you weeping? Whom are you seeking?" she mistakenly thought that the person speaking to her was the gardener. She said that she was looking for Jesus' body and if he would tell her where it was, then she would gladly take it away.

Jesus then called her name, saying, "Mary." She recognized the way he affectionately addressed her. He'd done this many times before. She then realized who it was that was speaking to her, and that Jesus was alive.

Mary called out, "Rabboni!" This was an Aramaic expression denoting Jesus as a respected teacher. She reached out to hold him. But he told her she couldn't. He had not yet ascended to his heavenly Father. This would occur later.[27]

Don't miss what Jesus said next to Mary. He told her to go to his disciples and tell them he was ascending to his Father and their Father. The disciples were now his brothers, and God was their Father. If you believe in Jesus, he is your big brother. And as big brothers do, he will protect you from those who desire to harm you.

And God is your personal, loving, kind, and caring Father. In the garden of Gethsemane, the night before Jesus went to the cross, he prayed to the Father and called him "Abba." It was an intimate, colloquial Aramaic expression that is best translated "Daddy." You can now know the heavenly Father in that way as well.

Perhaps you had an abusive, absent, or distant earthly father. Maybe you think if "God" is like your earthly father, you don't want anything to do with him. But the heavenly Father's original intent was for all children to have a loving and kind earthly daddy. Unfortunately, sin has corrupted everything in creation—even the family.

Jesus came from heaven to earth to reestablish the Father's original intent. He came to redeem humanity and to make all things new. He especially came to help you know the true character of his Father, who is also your Father.

God is your daddy. He loves you. He has a plan for your life—one filled with a future and a hope. He wants you to use the gifts he has given to you for his glory. He wants you to be all that he has planned for you to be. He loves you and believes in you.

Your heavenly daddy is very gracious, slow to anger, and abounding in great love. He is good. His steadfast love endures forever. He loves to rejoice over you and quiet your soul with his endless love.

The Father in heaven empathizes with your pain. Like any kind daddy, he hurts when you hurt. He cradles you in his arms and assures you all will be well. He heals your broken heart. When afflictions come, he gives the sufficient grace you need to bear the burden you are experiencing. He preserves your life.

He is a good heavenly daddy who loves and cares for you.

As your big brother who cares deeply for you, Jesus would not lie to you about something as important as this.

Go into the World

Today's Reading: John 20:16-23

HEARING GOD'S VOICE FOR TODAY:

"Jesus came and stood among them and said to them, 'Peace be with you...As the Father has sent me, even so I am sending you'... And when he had said this, he breathed on them and said to them, 'Receive the Holy Spirit. If you forgive the sins of any, they are forgiven them; if you withhold forgiveness from any, it is withheld.'"

* * *

J esus suddenly appeared to his disciples. They were hiding behind locked doors—fearful that they might be arrested and crucified as he had been.

He said to them, "Peace be with you." In fact, he said it twice. He wanted them to know that those who really believed that he had risen from the dead had no reason to fear anything. He wanted to give his followers a peace that conquers all fear. It's a peace that surpasses all understanding.[28]

Jesus also gave them a commission to go into the world. In doing so, he used the example of his own incarnation. In the same way the Father had sent him into the world, he was now sending his followers into the world.

Jesus does not want us to be removed from the world, being so heavenly minded that we are of no earthly good. Nor are we to be standing against the world, harshly judging all its sin from a distance.

Rather, we are to be in the world, lovingly influencing people so they can be transformed for God's glory. We are to be lights on a hill, loving the world with many good works. These good works will give the world reason to praise the heavenly Father.[29]

Jesus then breathed on his disciples and said, "Receive the Holy Spirit." Because the cross and the resurrection were now complete, the disciples could receive the gift of forgiveness. That was the reason Jesus had been sent from heaven to earth: for the forgiveness of sins.

Unless sins are forgiven, no human can see the face of God and live. The Father's highest priority was a personal relationship with his creation. But this relationship could not occur without the forgiveness of sins. If you want to spend eternity with the Father, you must first receive the forgiveness of your sins.

Jesus then gave all his followers this commission: Preach the gospel of forgiveness to the world. As the gospel is proclaimed and people believe it, they will be forgiven. But if the gospel is withheld, people will not hear about the opportunity to be forgiven.

As you share the gospel, keep these things in mind:

First, you have Jesus' presence with you, which also gives you his peace. This peace is not as the world gives it. The world's peace is merely the absence of conflict. Jesus gives you his personal presence, which grants you his perfect peace no matter what you are facing.

Second, Jesus sends you into the world. You are to live among the lost and do good works. Make the world a different and better place because you are living for Jesus in its midst.

Third, Jesus wants you to share the message about the forgiveness of sins with whomever you can. If you don't, how can people know about it? This commission is of eternal significance.

As the Father sent the Son into the world, now Jesus sends you into the world.

Your words and deeds will help transform it for his glory.

✳ ✳

Walk by Faith and Not by Sight

Today's Reading: John 20:24-31

Hearing God's Voice for Today:
"He said to Thomas, 'Put your finger here, and see my hands, and put out your hand, and place it in my side. Do not disbelieve, but believe.' Thomas answered him, 'My Lord and my God!' Jesus said to him, 'Have you believed because you have seen me? Blessed are those who have not seen and yet have believed.'"

✳ ✳ ✳

This is Jesus' second resurrection appearance in John's Gospel. During the first one, Thomas was not present. The disciples told him of the first appearance. Thomas was incredulous and said that unless he placed his finger into the mark of the nails in Jesus' hands, and in the place of the wound in his side, he would never believe.

So when Jesus appeared the second time, he invited Thomas to place his finger in his hands and side. He then lovingly exhorted Thomas not to doubt, but to believe. He wanted Thomas's unbelief to be destroyed and his faith to be strong.

Thomas responded simply, "My Lord and my God!" He chose faith. He chose to worship Jesus.

Thomas's response is a statement about Christ's deity. He proclaimed Jesus Lord and his personal God. He worshiped him. And Jesus accepted that worship. Thomas's conclusion was accurate. Jesus was his Lord and God. He was worthy of his worship.

Some people who try to disprove Jesus' claims to deity have suggested that Thomas's exclamation was simply one of astonishment. How unthinkable! If that were the case, then that means Thomas, a faithful Jew who knew the Ten Commandments, was using the Lord's name in vain.

Moreover, that suggestion is inconsistent with the flow of the story. Thomas's words were spoken to Jesus as a confession of faith in him as his resurrected Lord and personal God.

Jesus then adjured Thomas to walk by faith and not by sight. Faith is the evidence of things not seen. Indeed, Jesus' earthly followers who saw him alive and believed in him had a distinct advantage over those who have never seen, yet still believe. Because you believe without having seen Jesus, you are more blessed than they are. You understand fully what it means to walk by faith.

Walk by faith and not by sight. Trust that Jesus is who he says he is. Believe that his words do hold the key to eternal life.

Believe that Jesus is not only Lord and God over the universe, but he is also your personal Lord and God. He is closer than a brother. He is your intimate life companion.

His resurrection proves that he truly does rule over everything in the universe. Nothing is outside his dominion, power, and authority. All authority in heaven and on earth has been granted to him. Nothing happens to you that he doesn't oversee.

That means you don't need to worry about anything. The world is in his hands. Your day is in his hands. Don't be concerned about tomorrow. It has enough worries of its own.

Jesus is the resurrected Lord and God of all—including you!

✳ ✳

God Oversees Your Nothings

Today's Reading: John 21:1-3

HEARING GOD'S VOICE FOR TODAY:
*"Simon Peter said to them, 'I am going fishing.' They said
to him, 'We will go with you.' They went out and got
into the boat, but that night they caught nothing."*

✳ ✳ ✳

John wrote about Jesus' third resurrection appearance in his Gospel. There were many others, but the three John presented were the ones he chose to emphasize.

The disciples had returned to Galilee, where, as Mark noted, Jesus had commanded them to go and wait for him. Jesus had promised that he would go before them. If you are his disciple, that should be encouraging news for you. There is no place to where you go that he is not already there waiting for you.

The disciples waited patiently to see if Jesus would appear to them again. Peter was especially discouraged. He was dealing with his guilt, grief, and shame over having denied Jesus three times. He was in great need of the Lord's grace.

While the disciples waited, they started fishing again. That was natural for them to do. When someone is feeling uncertain about something in life, he often returns to what he knows he can do well. For some of the disciples, this meant their fishing business. That's what they had devoted their lives to when Jesus called them to follow him.

The disciples went out in a boat at night, which was the preferred time to fish. It was cooler, so the fish weren't swimming along the bottom. Also, when fish were caught at night, they could be sold quickly and easily in the market the next morning while still fresh. The disciples were skilled fishermen, and they knew what they were doing.

But this night, the disciples caught nothing. They repeatedly threw their nets over one side of the boat, then the other, but without success. They were completely shut out. Nothing worked for them.

At the time, the disciples didn't realize this truth: Jesus oversees all "nothings." This was all part of his perfect plan to help them receive his love and mission for them—especially Peter. As they saw Jesus make their nothing into something, their faith in him would increase.

In just a little bit, it would all make sense to them.

When nothing seems to be working for you, you need to trust that Jesus is the Lord of your nothings. When nothing seems to be happening in your life, trust him. It's not a surprise to him. He oversees all— even when nothing seems to be happening.

Jesus is using your nothings for a larger purpose. Sometimes he wants to exhaust you of all your human strength so you'll depend solely on him. Other times he doesn't want you to depend on what you do really well, but depend completely on him.

If it seems like nothing is working for you right now, rejoice! Trust him. He knows what he is doing. Faith continues to trust God when nothing seems be happening.

He is the Lord of your nothings.

✳ ✳

Don't Give Up

Today's Reading: John 21:4-6

Hearing God's Voice for Today:
"Jesus said to them, 'Children, do you have any fish?' They answered him, 'No.' He said to them, 'Cast the net on the right side of the boat, and you will find some.' So they cast it, and now they were not able to haul it in, because of the quantity of fish."

✳ ✳ ✳

The disciples were skilled fishermen. They had spent the entire night fishing, yet to no avail. They had caught nothing.

Jesus stood on the shore. It was early morning. As the sun peeked over the horizon, he called to them. They didn't recognize him at first. He called out to them, "Children." It was a term of endearment. His affection for all of them ran deep.

He then asked them if they had caught any fish. He knew they had caught nothing. That was part of the plan. He had willed for them to not catch anything. He had sovereignly decreed for all the fish to evade their nets.

He had a larger and better plan.

Jesus' disciples answered him and said that they hadn't caught anything. He told them to cast their nets on the other side of the boat.

The disciples wondered why they should obey some unknown figure instructing them from the shore. But they were tired. They knew they had nothing to lose. So they cast their nets on the other side of their boat.

When they did, they hauled in a large number of fish—too many for them to bring into the boat.

Do you see the purpose of all that happened here? This was similar to when Jesus fed the 5000.[30] With only five loaves and two fish, he fed them all—with 12 basketfuls of food left over. The disciples had been fishing all night and had caught nothing. But with one word, Jesus was able to supply a net so full of fish that they couldn't even bring them all on board the boat.

Do you understand? He is not a God of paucity, but of abundance. He wants to give exceedingly and abundantly beyond what you could ever hope or imagine. How great is his goodness stored up for those who fear him!

The Lord is not a miser, nor is he stingy. He is a giver. He enjoys blessing his children. When you delight in him, he loves to grant you your heart's desires. The Father so loved the world that he gave his only Son to die for you and give you eternal life. He gives strength to the weary and increases the power of the weak. He gives hope to those who feel nothing good is going to happen.

Your faith increases when you know what kind of God he really is. He is not trying to deny you life's enjoyment. He withholds no good thing from those who do what's right.

Don't give up. Keep persevering. Defeat happens only when you quit trying. Do what he says. Go to the other side of the boat and try again.

And experience the abundant blessings he has waiting for you there.

✳ ✳

The Two Faces of Grace

Today's Reading: John 21:7-14

HEARING GOD'S VOICE FOR TODAY:
*"Jesus said to them, 'Bring some of the fish that you have
just caught.' So Simon Peter went aboard and hauled
the net ashore, full of large fish, 153 of them. And
although there were so many, the net was not torn."*

✳ ✳ ✳

When Peter recognized Jesus on the shore, he swam to him. After he arrived, Jesus asked the disciples to bring him some fish. He wanted to fix breakfast for them and care for their every need.

Peter then went back to the boat and helped haul ashore the net full of fish. It should have torn, but did not. And these were not small fish, but large, healthy, and meaty ones.

How the Lord loves to lavish good gifts on his children. His steadfast grace gives unbroken nets and large fish. It knows no bounds. It never ceases and is new every morning. It is limitless for every day of life. Great is his faithfulness.

The disciples counted the huge haul. There were 153 fish in all. As fishermen, they always counted the number of fish caught before going to market. It was a way of comparing one day's work to the next, a way of computing success over weeks and months.

Some scholars have suggested that 153 also corresponds to the known number of different people groups at that point in human history. They wonder if this was Jesus' way of reminding his disciples of their calling to be fishers of men and to take the gospel to every people group in the world. To fish for people's souls was their primary calling.

There are two specific faces of grace we should note here.

First, Jesus wants to lavish his grace on you personally. It is an amazing grace. It is not only sufficient for everything you face in life, but is also given to you abundantly. He wants to give you unbroken nets of grace, full of large blessings.

Second, you are to be a messenger of his grace. You are a fisher of men. Jesus wants you to have a heart for the entire world to know him as Lord and Savior. He wants everyone, everywhere, to know about his abundant grace. Be local and global when you think about telling others of his love.

As you go, don't despair about anything. The Lord will supply your every need according to his heavenly riches. Your nets will not break. They are strong enough for your every need. And his fish aren't tiny, but large. How he enjoys giving you his good gifts!

Find ways to give his grace away to those around you and throughout the world. Just as you need his abundant grace, so do they. Don't get tired of doing what is good. When you persevere, at just the right time, you will reap a harvest of blessing. Don't give up.

When you fish for men, you are fulfilling one of the major reasons God created you. There is great joy in knowing you have helped introduce someone to Jesus and changed their eternal trajectory.

The angels in heaven rejoice when even one sinner comes home. Experience their joy as well as you obey Jesus' call to be his witness and make disciples of all the nations.

You are his ambassador to a dying world that needs his grace.

God's Purpose in Your Pain

Today's Reading: John 21:15-19

HEARING GOD'S VOICE FOR TODAY:
"Peter was grieved because he said to him a third time, 'Do you love me?' and he said to him, 'Lord you know everything; you know that I love you.' Jesus said to him, 'Feed my sheep.'"

✳ ✳ ✳

Jesus was doing spiritual heart surgery on Peter. He wanted Peter to know of his forgiveness for his denials. He desired for Peter to know that his love conquers all sin. He hungered for Peter's heart to believe he still had a great plan for his life.

Three times, Jesus asked Peter if he loved him. Three times, Peter responded in the affirmative. But the third time that Jesus asked this question, Peter showed great angst. Exasperated, he said, "Lord, you know that I love you." Jesus smiled inwardly, for Peter's heart was now prepared to receive Jesus' purpose for his life..

How did Jesus know Peter was ready? He knew because Peter had not only admitted his love for the Lord, but he also realized that Jesus knew everything. Peter trusted Jesus with all his being. That was essential—and the Lord knew Peter's heart belonged totally to him.

Jesus then commissioned Peter again to feed his sheep. He knew Peter would. He knew this disciple would take the message of forgiveness and faith that he had personally experienced and faithfully impart it to others.

That was Jesus' plan for Peter. In the upper room, Satan had asked permission to sift Peter like wheat.[30] As with Job, the Lord granted permission. There is nothing Satan can do to any of his followers unless

God permits it. He may be the devil, but he is God's devil. He is on a leash. He is not all-powerful.

Though this sifting would be exceedingly painful for Peter, it was Jesus' will for him. The pain would burn away his arrogance and impetuousness. It would prepare him for the plan Jesus had for him to be a primary pillar in the church.

It would also give Peter insights into essential eternal truths. His two New Testament letters were written primarily to a persecuted people. Because he had gone through his own deep pain, suffering, and disappointment, he could express the power of God's grace to those who needed great comfort and encouragement. The words he wrote would be life-giving words based on his own personal experience.

And the readers of his letters would have their faith profoundly encouraged.

There is purpose in your pain as well. The Lord keeps track of all your sorrows. He collects your tears in a bottle and records each one.[32] No tear that you shed is ever useless. No sigh in your soul goes unheeded.

How might God be using your troubles? The comfort you have received from him, you'll be able to give to others who are walking through a similar experience.[33] Like Peter, you'll be able to give to them the grace that you yourself received.

God causes all things to work together for good—even your painful problems.

If you don't believe that's true, read what Peter wrote in his two New Testament letters.

He will assure you there that it is true.

Total Obedience

Today's Reading: John 21:18-19

HEARING GOD'S VOICE FOR TODAY:

"'When you were young, you used to dress yourself and walk
wherever you wanted, but when you are old, you will stretch out
your hands, and another will dress you and carry you where you do
not want to go' (This he said to show by what kind of death he was
to glorify God.) And after saying this, he said to him, 'Follow me.'"

✳ ✳ ✳

Jesus had an important truth he wanted Peter to understand. When
Peter was younger, before being called by Jesus, he had complete freedom. He could go where he wanted and do whatever he desired. He
could dress himself the way he wanted without concern or worry. He
had total autonomy.

But that would all change because of his total devotion to the Lord.
A time was coming when he would be forced to stretch out his hands.
Jesus was referring to Peter's future crucifixion. Someone would come
and dress him to take him to his cross. He would be forced to go to a
place where did didn't want to go.

He would face martyrdom for following Jesus.

Legend suggests that Peter asked his executioners that he be crucified upside down. He didn't think himself worthy to die in the same
way his Lord had died. If true, it's a lovely affirmation of Peter's humility before he faced death.

Jesus then repeated to Peter what he had said when he first called
Peter to be his disciple: "Follow me." Once again, Peter was asked to
put down his fishing nets and obey what Jesus was calling him to do.

Peter would go to where Jesus wanted him to go, and obey the Lord completely until the day he died.

Jesus' call upon your life is equally total and compelling. He wants you to obey him no matter what the cost—even if it means death. You have decided to follow the Lord. You've chosen to love him more than anything else in this fallen world. There is no turning back.

Follow the Lord Jesus Christ. Go and make disciples of all the nations. Be his witness everywhere you go. Live as he tells you to live. Obey all that he commanded you to do. Joyful are those who obey him and search for him with all their hearts. When you obey him, you will remain in his love.

When you follow Jesus, he promises he will be with you always, even to the close of the age. He assures you that no weapon formed against you will prosper. He will stand beside you and be your protective shade. You will remain in eternal fellowship with him. He will always be at your right hand. You will not be shaken.

As you obey God and keep his covenant, you will find that you are his treasured possession. This should inspire you to be faithful to him until the end of your life, to always obey his command to walk in love.

For giving your life to him, your reward in heaven will be great. All your righteous deeds will be revealed. And you will hear the applause of heaven.

You will be greatly blessed and honored for all eternity.

Follow Me

Today's Reading: John 21:20-23

HEARING GOD'S VOICE FOR TODAY:

"When Peter saw him, he said to Jesus, 'Lord, what about this man?' Jesus said to him, 'If it is my will that he remain until I come, what is that to you? You follow me!'"

✳ ✳ ✳

Jesus had just told Peter that one day he would be asked to give his life in martyrdom for him. Peter turned around and noticed John following along. He asked, "Lord, what about this man?" He wanted to know if John would suffer martyrdom as well.

But that was not Jesus' plan for John. Yes, he would face persecution and pain, be arrested, and be exiled to the island of Patmos. Along with the Gospel of John, he would pen three letters to the churches. Plus he would reveal the insights Christ would give him into the end times in the book called Revelation.

Jesus would use John mightily. But John would not be martyred. He would die of old age after having faced his own trials.

Every person who follows Jesus goes through various trials. None of his disciples will be immune to them, though he is dealing with each one differently.

When you experience your trials, trust Jesus' plan for your life. Don't examine what he is doing with other people. Avoid the snare to compare. Only two things can happen when you do this, and both are bad. You'll either become proud or jealous. The Lord uses all his followers according to his perfect will. His plan for others is not his plan for you, and vice versa.

In fact, if you knew what Jesus was doing in other people's lives, you might stop making comparisons. You probably wouldn't want to go through what they are experiencing. Jesus gives each person the grace that is needed to face each trial he must face.

In your trial, Jesus is conforming you to his image. That's his will for you. As he lives in you, he wants you to become more and more like him. He desires that you be molded to his image, which is your hope of glory.

Jesus' plan for you is perfect. He has things for you to do on earth that only you can do. He commands you to walk in love. Blessed are those who hear God's Word and obey it without hesitation. Don't be just a hearer of his Word, but be one who insists on doing what it says.

Be faithful to his calling. Press on toward what he has asked you to accomplish.

The Lord has begun a great work in you. And he will be faithful to complete it.[34]

Christ is preparing you for eternity. He is burning off all your imperfections. He is making you pure, holy, and spotless through everything you experience in life. He is using everything that happens to you for your good and his glory.

He has a perfect plan for every single one of his followers. His plan for you is unique. No one else can do it but you. How he designs it to accomplish his will for you is up to him. Your job is to trust him no matter what. Believe that whatever is happening to you is exactly what you need so you can be conformed to his image.

Therefore, quit looking at what he is doing in others. Stop making comparisons.

What is that to you?

You follow him.

✳ ✳

Jesus Will Return

Today's Reading: John 21:24-25

HEARING GOD'S VOICE FOR TODAY:

*"This is the disciple who is bearing witness about these things, and
who has written these things, and we know that his testimony
is true. Now there are also many other things that Jesus did.
Were every one of them to be written, I suppose that the world
itself could not contain the books that would be written."*

✳ ✳ ✳

The disciple John was the one who wrote this Gospel. He always referred to himself as the disciple "whom Jesus loved." He was very humble and self-effacing. He wanted Christ alone to be the central character of this book.

You can trust that every single word written in the Gospel of John is true. John himself was an eyewitness to all that he wrote. He saw first-hand what the Lord did. He heard personally what Jesus spoke. He was a faithful, orthodox Jew and committed to never bearing false witness.

Notice John used the word "we" in his testimony. He was not the only eyewitness who saw all Jesus did and said. There were the other disciples, and hundreds of others, who followed, heard the Lord's teachings, and saw him alive after his death.

John concluded this book with the statement that Jesus had performed many other mighty works—so many that all the libraries of the world could not contain them all.

The Lord Jesus entered the world as a baby. He lived the perfect life no one could live. For 33 years, he obeyed perfectly all the righteous requirements of the law. Then he died on the cross, taking the wrath of his heavenly Father upon himself so you wouldn't have to face it. Then Jesus was raised back to life, proving that sin and death have no power over the Father's eternal grace.

All this was done so that you might inherit eternal life. It's the greatest act of love the world has ever known. And remember: If you confess with your mouth that Jesus is Lord, and believe in your heart that God raised him from the dead, you will be saved.[35] That's why the Word became flesh and dwelled among us. That's why Jesus came.

Today, Jesus sits at the right hand of the Father in heaven, awaiting the command to return to earth. On that day, he will judge the living and the dead. Those who believe in him will have everlasting life. Those who don't are doomed to everlasting punishment.

When Jesus returns, all wrongs will be made right. All hurts will be healed. Perfect justice will be enacted.

On that great day, Jesus Christ will make all things new. There will be a new heaven and a new earth. He is the Alpha and the Omega, the beginning and the end of all things. He will wipe away every tear from your eyes, and there will no longer be any death; there will no longer be any mourning, or crying, or pain.[36]

Until he returns, be faithful. Be sober and expectant. Let the Lord find you doing all that he has commanded you to do. Know him intimately. Live in peace, untroubled by fear or harm. Grow daily. Share in his divine nature. Escape the world's corruption caused by human desires. Go into the world with the good news and work to advance Christ's kingdom.

And trust Jesus with everything in your life.

He loves you.

Notes

✳ ✳ ✳

1. See Isaiah 26:3.
2. See 1 John 4:4.
3. See John 1:12.
4. These lines are based on the first stanza of "The Church's One Foundation," written by Samuel J. Stone, 1866.
5. See 1 Corinthians 2:9.
6. See Isaiah 40:8.
7. See Matthew 24:35.
8. Romans 5:3-5.
9. Matthew 28:19.
10. See Philippians 4:4.
11. See Jude 1:24.
12. See Joshua 1:8.
13. See Matthew 5:23-24.
14. See Matthew 27:19.
15. See Leviticus 4:2,13; 5:17.
16. See Matthew 28:18.
17. See Judges 8:23; 1 Samuel 8:7.
18. See 2 Corinthians 5:21.
19. See Exodus 20:12.
20. See Deuteronomy 17:6.
21. See Luke 24:13-35.
22. See Genesis 3:15.
23. See Psalm 22.
24. See Isaiah 53.
25. See Proverbs 18:10.
26. See Romans 8:1.
27. See Luke 24:51; Acts 1:9-11.
28. See Philippians 4:7.
29. See Matthew 5:16.
30. See John 6:1-13.
31. See Luke 22:31.
32. See Psalm 56:8.
33. See 2 Corinthians 1:4.
34. See Philippians 1:6.
35. See Romans 10:9.
36. See Revelation 21:4.

Other Good Harvest House Reading

✷ ✷ ✷

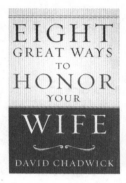

Eight Great Ways to Honor Your Wife
David Chadwick

God calls a husband to not only to love his wife, but to honor her. Sadly, honor is a missing ingredient in many marriages today.

When love and honor are practiced together, it takes the marriage to a whole new level. Join author David Chadwick as he shares eight great ways to make this happen:

trust her instincts	share your heart
be a man of God	respect her opinion
encourage her gifts	be a guardian and gardener
use words wisely	ask a certain question often

When a husband is honoring his wife, he will experience the very best of what God can do in a marriage relationship!

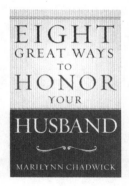

Eight Great Ways to Honor Your Husband
Marilynn Chadwick

A wife is uniquely able to honor her husband in ways no one else can. In *Eight Great Ways to Honor Your Husband*, author Marilynn Chadwick shares how a wife can show this special kind of love:

become strong	guard your home
believe the best	lighten his load
build him up	dream big together
fight for him	create a culture of honor

When a wife honors her husband, both of them experience new heights of fulfillment and intimacy—and others will see how beautiful the husband-wife union can be when it follows God's design.

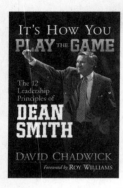

It's How You Play the Game
David Chadwick

Dean Smith won 879 games during his legendary career as a basketball coach—making him among the winningest coaches ever. He also won the respect and admiration of those who worked and played for him. What set him apart and made him so effective as a leader?

David Chadwick, who played on championship teams for Smith, provides an inside look at how Smith led and influenced others. You'll discover 12 principles that marked Smith's approach to leadership, including...

- put the team before the individual
- be flexible in your vision
- speak positive words
- make failure your friend
- commit yourself for the long haul

Whatever your calling as a leader—in business, athletics, ministry, or elsewhere—this book will equip you to play the game well...and win.